Zounds Demystified

Lyrics And Notes

by Steve Lake

Active Distribution/Bev Records 2013

Table Of Contents

Introduction

"I never tried once to drop out.
I just couldn't get in from the very start".

Zounds has been described as a political band. It has been labelled as squat rock, pop rock, peace punk, anarcho-punk, post-punk, psychedelic, punk-pop and a million other things. But those are just labels, I'm not that bothered what people call it really. I'm just pathetically grateful that anybody at all bothers to listen to it.

I never set out to make political statements, promote a point of view or publicise an ideology. In the days I started doing it I didn't even know what an ideology was. My point of view changes from day to day anyway. It did then and it does now, I change every 10 minutes. In that way I am the same as I ever was, so the songs contain a lot of contradictions and inconsistencies. Just like people's lives.

Someone came up to me at a gig recently and asked
'What should be done about the state of the world?'
How the fuck would I know? The longer I'm around the more mystified I become and the less I understand. All I can do is write songs and perform them.

I don't have a high opinion of people in bands, they are more unqualified than most to know what to do for the good of the world. If you had any desire to do anything for the planet you could work in medicine, human rights, education, the law, ethical industries, care, or many other useful endeavours.

Being in a band is shallow, narcissistic and ego driven; yet in some ways it is the highest calling. Music is the most mysterious and most affecting of all expressive activity. In the right circumstances it can be deeply moving, supremely joyful, deliciously sad, magnificently uplifting or painfully mournful. It is there at births, deaths, marriages and rites of passage. It marches us to war and accompanies us home. It soundtracks our victories and defeats. It tells stories and offers reflection and inspiration. It is in the church, the brothel, the sports game and the shopping mall.

Bands provide a vital function, but no one should have any illusion that they know any more than anyone else, or have an inside track on knowledge and wisdom. Musicians can sometimes conjure up and reflect the vagaries and extremes of life in a way that is sustaining and fulfilling, but more by accident than design. Never let a band tell you how to live or what to do. Many of them are idiots, I know I am. And I am a fucking genius compared to no-marks like Sting, Geldof and Bongo out of U2, all of whom have a Messiah complex and should be locked away for the sake of themselves and the community at large.

When I write songs I write from my own life, what is happening in the interior world of my head, and what leaks in from the outside environment.

Zounds lyrics contain a lot of politics. They also include satire, absurdism, surrealism, gut feeling, comedy, emotion, contradiction, confession, love, hate, celebration, comment, disgust, and a million other things. Zounds is not a political rock band, it's a cry for help.

This book contains lyrics and artwork from all of Zounds records. There are commentaries, background and notes relevant to the songs. Some of them are personal reminiscences about how we lived and what we were doing. Some place what we were up to in the wider social and political context of the day.

Zounds are often seen as an alternative or underground band. Part of a counter culture that has it's own history that exists at a tangent to mainstream thought and practice. But I never wrote for a specific audience, for a group or a sub-culture, a scene or a set. It has always been for anyone and everyone.

Despite that though, we were always on the outside of things, not through choice, it just worked out that way. Like it says in the song, we just couldn't get in. There is a lot of bollocks talked about outsider art. We were/are outsiders, not out of choice and not in the Hollywood 'rebel without a haircut' mould, but people who really couldn't get in. We were always the outsiders, even on the outsider scene.

"All the world cannot be wrong it must be me I don't belong".

Pre-historic times

Free festivals were something else in the 1970s and early 1980s. The first one I went to was in 1973, the Third Annual People's Free Festival in Windsor Great Park.

The key events for me though took place the following year in 1974. Steve Burch and I took some really strong acid and spent a day at the festival having the most fantastic trip, all sunshine, music, colours, laughing and cosmic possibilities. At the height of the trip a hippie approached us and asked us to sign a petition. The unlikely proposition was something akin to demanding the Queen ban the police from entering the site and order them to stop harassing the festival goers. Can't really remember the details, I was tripped off my head after all. My reply to the hippie was something inane like 'we're the ones breaking the law and not supposed to be here'. At which point, with a twinkle in his eye and a conspiratorial air in his voice he insisted 'We can go anywhere'.

The innocuous comment was an epiphany for me of epic and cosmic proportions. I am not sure such a thing can be experienced without the aid of psychedelic drugs. My head exploded, my body melted, sound and colour fused, my senses seemed to be connected to everything. I was elated, inspired, ecstatic, and had all the trans-cendent insight associated with deep spiritual revelation. It really was like a religious experience. All the standard psychedelic stuff, even drug experiences can be cheap and clichéd. But it just seemed so obviously true and profound that it turned my world upside down and I never thought the same way again.

Maybe that is an example of the permanent damage drugs can do. I never recommend that people take drugs and I never recommend they don't. Some people have an incredible tolerance to drugs, not me, I am very breakable and too fragile for prolonged drug use. I never regret it, but I couldn't go back there.

At the end of the long, lysergic day and the mind-blowing intensity of the trip, Steve and I decided to go back to my grandparent's house and play records. By leaving when we did we missed a violent, heavy and unnecessary dawn invasion of the site by the Thames Valley

Police. Hippies, including a pregnant woman, were truncheon-whipped and beaten up. There was no provocation for this and the brutality of it came as something of a surprise, and not just to the hippies. It was in the papers for a week. While these latter day flower-children were not held in high regard by the rest of society, I don't think they were perceived as deserving that kind of treatment. The dawn raid and the tripped out revelation really started to harden my attitudes to everything. It was quite a simple equation for me, on one hand you had a group of people going out into the countryside trying to have a nice time, coexist peacefully, play music and celebrate life in a free, non-commercial, co-operative, joyful, way; on the other hand the forces of the State, the government, the Queen and the commercial world wanted to descend upon them and destroy their festival with brutal violence, inherited privilege, cold insensitivity, perverse hatred and a certain measure of jealousy.

I didn't have to choose sides, I was already in the first camp, and I now started to get an insight into how cruel and viciously petty the straight world could be. How the interests of the few were privileged over the interests of the many. How those interests were backed up with the full might of the law, a law that was enforced with violence or the threat of violence. Eventually all power comes out of the barrel of a gun, the blade of a sword, the crunch of a boot or the smash of a fist. Things started to make sense, and a creeping disillusionment with society and the individuals and groups that made it up set in. It was realisations like this that made it impossible to take acid after a while. When I was a naive, junior freak who felt everybody could be good and had the potential for saintliness it was fine. As soon as I realised there was a grimy, nasty side to people that seemed incurable I couldn't do it anymore.

British justice – the best money can buy

All of these revelations were further compounded some months later when Debby Webb suggested we spend two weeks attending the trial of Ubi Bill Dwyer, the man who more than anyone else was responsible for inspiring and realising the Windsor Free Festival. He had been arrested for a number of offences in connection with the event, and as Berkshire County Court was located near where we lived in Reading we were able to attend everyday. I was about to learn a few more lessons about the British Justice System.

I can't remember all the details of the case at this far distant

8

point, you can find them on the internet if you're interested, but I do remember that Bill Dwyer presented himself in an honest, open, dignified and courteous manner throughout. His arguments were reasonable and believable. On the other hand the police witnesses were unbelievable, dull-witted and had an air of dishonesty that was obvious and palpable. Even the stereotypical, crusty old judge seemed sympathetic to Dwyer and incredulous at the police evidence. Watching the archaic and arcane theatre of a British court hammered home the inequities and power relationships on which British life was based. Bill Dwyer was admittedly eccentric and unconventional, but he had a vision based on peace, love and understanding. He tried to do something that was selfless and beautiful. He may have even been a little crazy, but he was harmless and full of goodness and generosity. Yet he was hammered by the state and its agents and thrown into prison. They called it justice but it seemed most unjust to me. I cried when they dragged him roughly from the court to prison. It was so patently unfair and so needlessly heavy. What good would it do society to have this gentle, kindly man locked in a prison, it was ridiculous and pathetic.

There was another significant event for me at the trial. Debby and I noticed there were some other wayward freaks in the public gallery. Predictably we ended up gravitating towards each other. It turned out to be a posse from London who were running the legendary underground newspaper International Times. The prime mover was the anarchist playwright Heathcote Williams, a real doyen of the British underground movement and a man who went on to do lots of fantastic stuff. He was one of those well-bred aristocratic types who had thrown it all in to be a hero of counter-cultural Bohemia. He was really inspiring and Debby and I became street sellers for International Times. I remember walking round Watchfield Festival in a sea of laughter, trying to sell the paper on acid, repeatedly screaming out 'murder, rape buggery', the headline emblazoned across the front page in true tabloid style. Those hippies always had a real cool sense of humour.

Flower punk - Watchfield 1975

Watchfield was the alternative site for the Windsor festival in 1975. It was an old airfield and had been given to the hippies for the festival. It is a measure of how much controversy there had been at the previous years police brutality that the Government would provide and sanction a site for a free festival, because the festivals really were anarchy in action. That meant that there was some incredible, mind-blowing things going on, but it also meant that there was a lot of disturbed, unpleasant and weird behaviour happening too. These festivals could be very, very big, and although they were often organised through the London underground's radical movers and shakers, loads of different types of people would turn up. Hippies, bikers, heavy metal kids, Krishna people, Jesus people, straights, anyone wanting to break loose, taste a bit of freedom and have a hedonistic sabbatical from the strictures of everyday life. There was generosity and sharing and co-operation, but there was also selfishness, exploitation and anti-social activity. There were people marginalised by society with mental illness, learning-difficulties and a host of needs and complexes, plus a fair sprinkling of drug casualties.

The aircraft hangers at Watchfield became sulphurous caves faintly illuminated by piles of burning rubber tyres belching out acrid and poisonous smoke. Bikers would drive their machines through the half-light and god help any stumbling wreck that got in the way. Black smoke, toxic fumes, bad speed and no sanctions could lead to some pretty hairy situations. On the whole though things got worked out, stuff happened and mostly everyone had fantastic times.

The most significant thing for me at Watchfield though was the debut gig of precocious, young psychedelic upstarts and junior-Gong-wannabes Here and Now on the Polytantric Stage. They got a massive audience, largely because they had a synthesiser player called Twink. Twink was also the name of the ex-drummer of The Pink Fairies, undisputed kings of the British underground and free gig scene. Most of us just assumed this was his new band and Here and Now did nothing to clear up the confusion. The band rose to the occasion admirably and played all night, though I'm not sure I actually remember the performance. The important thing about them was that they then took over the mantle of 'free festival house band'. Without them the scene might have been consigned to the dustbin of history. They went on to provide the impetus, music and attitude that drove the festival scene and its associated life style on into the uncertain future. They were also instrumental in providing gigs, equipment, opportunity and encouragement to Zounds, The Mob and The Astronauts. We all met through Here and Now.

Although I had been playing with a fifties style rock n roll band in down-market brothels and biker events before this, Watchfield was the first proper 'alternative gig' I played. I did it with the phenomenal Tim Rundall, a.k.a. 'Slim Tim Slide'. Exhibiting a display of uncanny prescience for what was just around the corner we did a version of Frank Zappa's 'Flower Punk'. Tim ended up playing with Mick Farren, the Pink Fairies and various members of the MC5. The circle was complete, respect to Tim, love him.

Stonehenge 1975 - 81

Stonehenge Free Festivals were something else again! So many trips and traumas and tangents. I'd been going since about 1975 and Zounds had played every year from 1978 to 1981. I never went again after that. Penny Rimbaud, the drummer and leader of Crass, has written extensively about the genesis of the festival and it is well worth a read.

Stonehenge was a big festival and would stretch on for a week around the summer solstice. The weekends were always massive, not just hippies and weirdos, but anyone out for a bit of hedonism in the strange and ancient Wiltshire countryside. In those days the Stones weren't caged in so on the dawn of the solstice we'd all troop down there and mill about expectantly, smoking joints and chillums and pipes. No problems. The druids would do their shtick. Self styled king of the Hippies Sid Rawles would babble incomprehensible nonsense, then we would go back to the campsite and .... eat? Did we eat in those days? I don't remember eating.

At Stonehenge the main stage was usually conjured up by Here and Now or Polytantric or some other bunch of mysterious freaks. Grant Showbiz, who went on to produce The Smiths, The Fall, Billy Bragg and a host of others, usually colonised and organised the stage in his role as Here and Now sound guy/manager/producer/ mentor/guru/whatever. He would sit at the mixing desk, always with a microphone, directing operations like some long suffering, benevolent dictator, keeping watch, over-seeing everything and directing his carefully honed cynicism at hoards of stoned, child-like musicians trying to get on stage.

There was one fateful occasion in 1979 when it was decided

a collection should be taken from traders and vendors who had pitched up at the site hoping to make a bit of dough from the congregated hoards. Most of them were happy to bung a few quid in the kitty to keep the generator going and the bands playing. After all, if it all stopped and everyone went home there would be nobody to make money from. One hot-dog seller refused to pay and was unnecessarily arsey about it. Grant was somewhat incensed at the lack of co-operation and rude belligerence of this petty-capitalist fuck-wit. With his dander up and full of revolutionary zeal Grant took to the stage and gave an emotional, and completely justified, tirade about how the hot dog guy was exploiting the people. He explained that the miscreant was happy to take money from the assembled masses but was completely unprepared to give anything back or contribute in any way. Grant declared that he was going over to the vendor to tell him to contribute or get off the site, and that all the festivalgoers should go with him. If the hippies are united they will never be defeated. Sadly the hippies were too stoned to act on the call to collective action. The bikers at the festival though were moved by Grant's inspirational words and accompanied him to the offending van. Proceedings then got a bit out of hand and the biker's sense of injustice was such that they trashed the van, turned it over, and then chased the exploiter from the site. I don't think it was quite how Grant envisaged it, but it was effective.

Grant Showbiz was (and still is) an inspiring and charismatic figure who was a major force in the free-gig scene. He is someone who, while making his mark in the straight music-biz, has always been involved in grass roots, independent, community music making. His enthusiasm for life and music and good vibes is inspirational, definitely one of the good guys. As well as playing on the main stage, Zounds usually hustled up some small generators and amps and speakers to play in other parts of the site. Somehow everything got provided, no one paid for anything. That was what was so great about it. It is often said that people have to be compelled to 'work' or nothing would get done. My experience at places like Stonehenge was that some people actually want to do stuff and don't want to just sit around taking from others. Bands played, sound systems and stages and generators got provided, people organised free food, dug toilets, collected wood, went on water runs. Yes there was some right fucking drongos there as well, but that is the human race for you, there are all bloody sorts. The thing was, we did it for ourselves and for each other, and it was far-fucking-out.

1981 and all that

When Zounds first started playing at Stonehenge we were in our full-on improvising/Krautrock/West Coast/freak-out phase. Every year we got slightly more focused and song oriented. By the last year we were a stripped-down three-piece with short songs and a much more direct approach. We had also gone from being a loose, spontaneous outfit to being a group with records in the Independent charts. Times had changed. Punk bands had played Stonehenge before, memorably the wonderful ATV, led by Mark Perry. Despite what your history books tell you Mark Perry was the man with more of a claim than anyone else for 'inventing British punk rock'.

In 1981 a few of the bands associated with Crass decided to play, not just us and free festival veterans The Mob, but Crass themselves, Annie Anxiety and Flux Of Pink Indians. It was all very different to previous festivals though. The details are cloudy, but I remember it was weird turning up to find the Crass party and loads of black clad, punky, spike-tops mingling with the usual crew of latter day hippies, bikers, freak-outs and people with only the flimsiest grip on reality as most of us perceive it. As far as I remember Flux Of Pink Indians played, or it may have been the Mob, or maybe even both, then we stepped up. There were a lot of bikers in the crowd and they really didn't like what they were seeing and hearing. They started shouting for rock n roll and the atmosphere became very menacing. The sky and the mood were both starting to get dark as we took the stage. The shouting had become more aggressive and a few scuffles broke out in the crowd. I was pretty nervous, as was Joseph. Laurence tended not to be so phased by these sort of things. Then bottles started to rain down on to the stage and the cries of 'fuck off' and 'rock n roll' intensified.

OK, it wasn't quite the post-punk Altamont, but it felt like it could be as bottles, fists and boots started flying. The generator was attacked and went dead, amps started toppling over and vicious fighting broke out between bikers and punks. It was all very unexpected. Despite many differences of philosophic outlook with bikers, I always saw them as freewheeling, anarchic outsiders, worthy of respect and with a shared commitment to getting out of it and a desire to live outside the rules of everyday, bourgeois morality. But then, I always was a hopelessly deluded, romantic fool. Some of the bikers expressed the view that 'their festival' had been taken over by punks and had to be stopped. As I had been playing there for years and organised stages, generators, publicity, water runs and wood runs, and as members of Crass had been involved on an intimate level with getting the whole thing off the ground in the first place, I took great exception to this. I didn't bother trying to raise my concerns with the biker crowd though, they seemed a bit too cross to discuss 'people's solidarity' and tactical alliances between the various dispossessed sects on the fringes of mainstream society.

Away from the stage area all was sunshine and light and everyone else was oblivious to the mayhem taking place at the other end of the site. So I went off to a distant corner of the festival and peacefully smoked dope with a bunch of squatters from Islington and Hackney. As far as I remember a biker band took over the stage and played greaser classics such as 'Route 66' and 'Bye Bye Johnny' into the early hours. Zounds could have done that!

Free gigs

Free festivals led to the 'free gig' scene. This was pioneered by Here and Now and taken up by Zounds, The Mob, The Astronauts, The Androids Of Mu and not many others. The main inspirations for this were three visionary alumni of the Here and Now entourage. Charismatic drummer and singer Kif-Kif La Batteur (later to find fame as Keith Dobson with the great avant-noise wonders World Domination Enterprises), the aforementioned Grant Showbiz, and visionary, drunken poet and charmer Jonathan 'JB' Barnet (latterly the instigator and organiser of the Portobello Film Festival).

Kif-Kif and Grant left Here and Now in 1978 and Jonathan and Kif-Kif set up Fuck Off Records and Tapes. It would have been a shoestring operation if they had had as much as a shoestring. The pair put on gigs and released tapes of the burgeoning weirdo, underground bad-music scene in West London (and far distant cousins like the Instant Automatons from Scunthorpe). Along with Grant they put on endless free gigs at Portobello's Acklam Hall and Meanwhile Gardens in Westbourne Grove. They organised free tours for the Fuck Off stable of misfits and trawled some pretty extreme and confrontational sounds around the country. Then JB had the notion that Zounds, The Mob, The Astronauts and The Androids Of Mu should undertake a nationwide free tour in a bus under the banner of 'Weird Tales'. Laurence and I spent two weeks at Debby Webb's house phoning all the main rock clubs and college venues. Our mission was to persuade them to take four unknown bands with no records out, for no money and no entrance fee. The bands would take a collection and the venue would get the profits from the bar. A load of places went for it and we secured gigs in all the standard music venues of the day.

Organising the tour did lead to a bit of hassle over the telephone bill sadly. Debby was living with a load of hardcore, anarchist activists, but they all had jobs, or were students or something. Dave Morris, who was later to become the hero of the McLibel trial, was always round there fermenting sedition and writing leaflets. Being incredibly naïve and only marginally connected to real life, it didn't occur to us that people paid bills. We never did, so we assumed that if they had a phone they were getting it for free, especially with them being anarchists and all. That wasn't the case though and they ended up with a huge phone bill. We didn't go round there again for ages. We weren't into ripping people off, but we reasoned that as our music was about to fuel a new age of peace, togetherness and plenty for all, our wage slave anarchist compadres would get their reward when an era of paradise was realised here on earth. Which I figured would only be two hit singles and a killer album away. As it transpired the new age never really happened so I guess we still owe them.

Many of the bands I have known and played in seem to possess the unrealistic and unfeasible belief that they can simultaneously be bigger than the Beatles, save the world from ecological disaster, bring about world peace, feed the hungry, comfort the dispossessed and find a really cool girlfriend. Their qualifications for this are a combination of limited musical ability, a set of samey three-chord songs, the power of the will, and a messianic, egomaniacal sense of self-deception (this is probably as a result of over compensating for even deeper feelings of self-doubt and worthlessness, but we'll have to consult Doctor Freud for the answer to that one).

Once the tour was all set up and ready to go I left the band and hitched to Italy with my friend Derek Smith. We had somehow got the idea into our heads that we were Woody Guthrie and Cisco Houston, and that we must light out for new territory, spreading our message to the oppressed people of the world. I'm not sure what our message was, I think it might have been sex, dope, guitars and the greater glorification of ourselves. After visiting my ex-girlfriend in Italy I was going to hitch round the world busking, picking fruit and generally being free and spontaneous.

After a month or so of sponging off my ex-girlfriend, living without money, failing to get even the most basic grasp of the Italian language and being generally clueless about anything, I got homesick and started really missing my band. I went back to London with my tail between my legs and had to endure the band regaling me with tales of glorious gigs, exciting tour adventures, how well the new bass player fitted in, the hedonistic delights of post-gig revelries and the wonderful camaraderie experienced by all. It was enough to make you sick. After all the effort and energy I put in to organising the tour it had been a raving success and I had missed it. I also felt there was a certain amount of resistance to having me back in the band, but somehow I crow-barred my way back in, inveigled myself back into the Kings Cross squat I had been living in previously, regained the reins of Zounds, and picked up where I left off. At once I decided that having missed out on the first tour I would organise another one with the same bands.

Weird Tales round 2

Charly Records was, and still is, a successful and respected re-issue label that had signed ex-Soft Machine and Gong front man Daevid Allen. Allen was a friend and collaborator of Here and Now and got them signed to the label too.

Jonathan Barnett was still roadie-ing for Here and Now as well as pursuing his various other interests with Kif-Kif and Grant. He told one of the office juniors that Mark Mob and myself were doing some stuff for Here and Now and that Charly wanted us to share his office and phone-lines to book some gigs. The office junior was basically scamming himself, using Charly resources to promote some pointless Mod Revival band he was managing. So Mark Mob and I would sneak up the stairs about mid-day and spend a few hours hustling gigs while having the piss taken out of us by Mr Mod Revival. Thank you Charly records for unknowingly providing resources in pursuance of the free gig scene. You will get your reward in hell.

The tour itself got off to a cracking start at the Raindrop Club, a squatted pub in Frestonia, an area around West London's Freston Road that was essentially 'squat city', and had declared itself a free, autonomous, anarchist community. I don't think it was ever recognised by the State, the police or even the local council, but it was a happening place and can regularly be seen in old episodes of 'Minder', where it was used as the back drop for car chases. Zounds played 'War' for the first time that night and went down a storm. I remember Grant disbelievingly proclaiming to all and sundry in his extrovert and attractively camp manner, 'Oh my god I don't believe it, Zounds actually have fans'. Then he moaned on, in an equally loud voice, about how he tried to buy the Mob tape but got the Zounds one by mistake, and it just droned on interminably for hours. And to think we still let him produce our demo tape for Crass!

I had received my dole cheque that day and spent it all on drinks for anyone and everyone. My aim that evening was to spend all my money at the Raindrop Club and go on tour with nothing. We would live or die by what we collected at gigs, and trust in our righteousness and the fairness of the people to contribute something in return for the music and vibes we were bringing to their town. Of course, not everyone shared my enthusiasm and I soon learnt that while I was living off scraps, other people sensibly brought money and dope and were fairing rather better than me. The Astronauts didn't show for most of the gigs, so on the bus it was Zounds, The Mob, The Androids of Mu, Grant Showbiz, a baby, two dogs who hated each other, driver and master mechanic Tim, and a couple of other likely lads. One of those likely lads was the archetypal, hard-drinking, blues playing, Scottish roadie called Mac who seemed to be a fixture of the Frestonia music scene. Mac and I ended up hanging out together quite a lot on that tour. There were some fantastic gigs and some intense experiences.

Manchester Poly was especially memorable. A load of underage kids turned up and weren't allowed in, so Zounds found a fire escape on one of the upper floors and opened it up so the juvenile hoard could climb up and get in to the gig. Sometime in 2008 I got an email from a guy saying he was one of the people we let in at that gig, and it was the best night of his life. I got ridiculously drunk and The Fall came to watch the gig. Could life get any better? I ate a jar of mayonnaise later that night and shared a bottle of Whiskey Mac with my new Scottish friend. I went to sleep, awaking a short while later with an overwhelming urge to vomit. I grabbed an empty pint glass and filled it with regurgitated mayonnaise, whiskey mac and beer. Not sure how long it had been since I had actually eaten. What didn't fit in the pint glass went over my clothes. I only had the clothes I was wearing, a white boiler suit with the phrase 'I'm hungry and I need a drink' emblazoned across the back in magic marker. The next day I managed to a have bath in the Poly halls of residence. It was the first time in over a week I took my clothes off. But I had to put them back on again and didn't take them off for the rest of the tour. Hard to believe now.

JB had turned up in Manchester to join the bill with his cosmic/prog/sci-fi heavy metal outfit 'The Entire Cosmos'. The drummer of that band was Joseph Porter who unbeknownst to all would be the Zounds drummer inside a couple of months. We had nothing booked the day after Manchester Poly so JB decided to trawl the pubs of Moss Side and get us a gig that evening. The only thing to be had was a talent show in a scruffy working class pub on a nondescript 1970s council estate. They had no entries for the competition so we agreed to take it over and put on our own talent show with the Weird Tales bands. The £50 prize, or what ever it was, would go into the tour kitty. We all played covers, and various combinations of people did a turn. I smarmed my way through it as compere and a merry time was had by all. The Mob won by popular vote with their stellar version of 'Get It On' or some such T. Rex confection. The locals loved it and we didn't get beaten up.

The Entire Cosmos hitched back to London the next day. I think JB asked for some money for the journey. My memory is that, despite his initial inspiration for the tour, and despite his getting the gig at the talent show, he was refused any money. Beaten and bedraggled they set out for the motorway. We probably only had enough money for petrol to the next gig, but I still felt we were being mean. But I had nothing myself, and the collections weren't stretching as far as we would have liked.

There were some other memorable gigs, Wolverhampton Poly stands out. A recording of it eventually turned up on the Internet and is quite easily accessible for free download. It is typical of those gigs. Grant providing a running commentary through his mic at the mixing desk, Laurence making cheery, un-rock n roll observations to the audience during the Zounds set, me losing patience and making snide and unkind remarks about Laurence in response,

Curtis of the Mob being belligerent on stage. Long gaps in the music while collections were taken.

I had a huge row with Zounds guitar player Nick Godwin that night. I loved Nick and I loved his fluid, original playing. He was the one that really pushed the Can influence in the beginning. He was into all sorts of extreme and crazy music, and he and I would make strange tape collages that we would plaster all over the Zounds tapes we sold at gigs. Zounds could just as easily have become a total weird-out, avant-rock band. We could have gone in a whole heap of different directions. Despite our mutual love of the experimental stuff, Nick and I were on different paths at that point. We were both getting much more song oriented. But while I was looking to play faster, harder and simpler, Nick was getting jazzier, softer and more complex. It came to a head at the Wolverhampton gig and we had a right old shouting match. I refused to play one of his songs, telling him it was too wet and wimpy (even though I had written the words to it). The whole thing was horrible. I was really drunk again. We had a bit of an emotional make-up later at the gig, but essentially that was it for him in Zounds. At the end of the tour Nick left the band, and although we played and recorded together a lot after that, the resentment was too much for him and he came to hate me and probably always will. I also had a fight with Curtis that night. We had always been a bit wary of each other. We never really made much of a connection for some reason. Though he is actually a very nice person, and a really great bass player, it's probably something wrong with me. At the end of the night he was standing next to a long trestle table on which was piled a couple of hundred beer glasses. He started throwing them one by one at a wall, and they were shattering all over the floor. He was as drunk as I was. I stepped in and tried to get him to stop. He wouldn't, so we had a bit of a tussle and ended up on the ground. Somehow I found myself sitting on top of him and repeatedly banging his head against the floor screaming 'I hate violence'. He must have been very, very drunk though, because he was a tough little Somerset farm boy and could have beaten my soft, home-counties frame to a bloody pulp if he wanted to. Curtis and I have finally spoken about 'our issues' and happily buried the hatchet. You know, we were all very fucked up by various things, and the surprising thing is that there weren't a lot more outbreaks of violence.

As the tour was winding to a close hardship set in and it all started to become a bit grim and petty. I see now what the real problem was, Grant had to leave the tour, possibly after the Wolverhampton gig. With him gone it all fell apart. It seemed to me that one or two of the richer hippies in the entourage were doing fine. Also those who had some measure of maturity were OK. I was neither and I started to hate it. No regular food, those with dope wouldn't share it, not with me anyway. I was feeling alienated from most of the party and it probably went on a little too long. One day near the end of the tour we broke down on the motorway. Somehow we got hold of a load of potatoes and Curtis was cooking them on the bus. Then we found a cigarette butt in the food. I thought Curtis had thrown it in and we had another set to. I remember roaches, dog food and all sorts of unsavoury stuff getting thrown in the already unappetising dish, rendering it totally inedible. It seems I was totally wrong in thinking Curtis was the culprit. But memory is so unreliable there might not be a word of truth in any of this. Many of us were very troubled people and did many weird and unadvisable things, I know I did.

At Letchworth the carburettor of the bus stopped working. Tim, the driver and genius mechanic, managed to rig-up a tube that went from the petrol tank into the bus. Someone had to sit by Tim, constantly pouring petrol from a can into a funnel, which fed into the tube and into the engine. One stray spark from the joint Tim was smoking and we would have all gone up in flames. That was also the gig where the P.A. started to go wrong and Mark Mob got badly electrocuted on stage, his pale skin and frizzy blonde hair turning blue and sizzling with electricity. Luckily the power cut out quite quickly but Mark was thrown to the floor and pretty dazed for a while. Thankfully he was spared to carry on, but it was very frightening, especially as we still had a few gigs to go and we all had to continue to play through the deteriorating P.A.

You boys and girls should hook up with Crass

We noticed that most of the places the tour visited had posters announcing that Crass and Poison Girls were either about to play the venue, or had just been there before us. At Bishop Stortford, a really good gig with a very enthusiastic audience, the promoter started going on about how well he thought we would get on with Crass. He reckoned we were quite similar in outlook, and that we should get together with them. Frankly none of us knew anything about Crass, though the Poison Girls seemed like an interesting band. The promoter gave us the address of Crass, and like some cheesy Hollywood movie, our bus broke down a couple of miles from their home. A fine old English farmhouse on pasture that doubled as a nuclear submarine tracking station. There were big aerials all around the house, it was like something from a John Wyndham novel.

Mark Mob, Laurence, Cosmic and Corina from The Androids Of Mu, and myself wandered down there and had a splendid evening, chatting and laughing and comparing notes. They were obviously on a different mission to us, but we had a lot of stuff in common. Most of them were quite a bit older than us but that wasn't a problem. They were obviously pretty self-sufficient in commercial terms, where as we were just pretty. They gave us loads of records and we talked about recording for their label. Eventually they gave us a lift back to the bus, helped fix it, and off we went.

The last gig was in Slough. The bus gave up for good and was abandoned somewhere in the badlands of Essex. Someone came up with a transit to get people, dogs, baby and equipment back to London. I'd had enough. I hitched back to London with Goojey Pete, a friend who somehow appeared on the last leg of the tour. The next day I hitched to the gig in Slough where we discovered that Here and Now had turned up. They claimed that they were booked to play and knew nothing about the Weird Tales crew being similarly engaged. Seemed like too much of a coincidence, especially considering how intimately the bands were connected. As we were using the Here And Now P.A. they would have had no equipment to play through had we not turned up. Thank fuck it was the last gig of the tour. We were all fucked up, out of money and out of luck. Nick decided to leave the band and Laurence and I felt we needed to ditch Judge, our drummer at the time. We really wanted to harden up the sound, and Judge was quite a light drummer, good but too light for what we wanted. We recorded a Grant Showbiz produced demo at the squatted Street Level Studio in Bristol Gardens and then said goodbye to Judge. In came Joseph Porter, a friend and fan of the Mob. He had followed his heroes up from Yeovil to get in a band himself. He was the perfect choice, a totally unique and marvellous character who was learning about everything fast.

01 CAN'T CHEAT KARMA

One - Two - Three - Go
I've got an ego
It won't let me go
What am I gonna do?
A - B - C - D
Paranoia's killing me
I'm dying on my aching feet
What a way to go
Roll up - Roll up
People always stroll up
Say "Why don't you grow up?"
No thank you!
Big cats, small cats
Some cats are fat cats
Those cats are bad cats
What we gonna do?

There's an awful lot of people in the world today
There's an awful lot of trouble on the streets these days
And it doesn't seem to matter what you do or say
If a change is gonna happen got to help it on its way

A change is gonna come before too long I know
Peace has gotta come, well, I could be wrong I know
But I just don't know what I can do

You don't trust me and I don't trust you
I bet you wish you did and I know I do
Why have you got secrets cos I know you have
If you've got something to hide then it must be bad

A change is gonna come before too long I know
Peace has gotta come, well, I could be wrong I know
But I just don't know what I can do

Can't Cheat Karma

Crass records - Penny Rimbaud - Auditioning at
Dial House - Session drummers - Stupid lyrics

When it was decided we were going to record for Crass Records we agreed to do the songs 'War' and 'Subvert'. Penny Rimbaud (the charismatic de-facto leader of Crass) wanted another song for the record. It was an era when value for money was often measured in quantity rather than quality. So we went along to Crass H.Q. in Epping to audition a potential third song for the anarcho-supremo. I wanted to do a song called 'I Just Wanna Be Loved', but Penny thought it was a piece of meaningless poppy, punky fluff. I didn't think so because I really did want to be loved, and I felt very unlovable.

Frankly we didn't have many songs at the time. Zounds seemed to change personnel every 5 minutes so the newish line up with Joseph had a very limited repertoire. Laurence suggested we try 'Can't Cheat Karma'. I said no! But Penny's eyes instantly lit up and he insisted we play it. He liked the title. (It is a catchy title, and in later years it became something of a catch phrase for Jarvis Cocker). We launched into it, reluctantly on my part. Penny was smitten and decided immediately that would be the third song, he didn't need to hear any more. These anarchists can certainly be decisive when they want to be!

At first I was surprised he took to it. The idea of 'karma' seemed a bit hippiefied and slightly 'spiritual' for the militantly atheistic Crass. What I was forgetting though was that essentially Penny was, and always will be, an unreconstructed beatnik, and beatniks always had a bit of a liking for eastern mysticism. Anyway, it was only the B-side, or so I thought. Once the record was finished and released we discovered Penny had made it the A side. There he goes again, leading from the front.

In the studio, session drummers and selling out

We recorded the single with Penny and his old university buddy John Loder producing. It was fun working with Penny, he is a funny and interesting guy. I always liked him. He'd been around the block a few times and had a wealth of anecdotes and opinions, all of which he could spin out in an engaging and hilarious manner. I was a bit sceptical when he claimed to have met the Beatles on 1960s pop programme 'Ready Steady Go'. But the evidence is there on youtube for all to see. Penny sent a picture in to a competition and Lennon chose it as the winner.

I couldn't work out Loder though, from what I've heard no one could. Laurence still goes on about his refusal to inform us about our publishing rights, and still wonders why he never sent us any statements, or paid us more than a couple of hundred quid after the record came out and scraped into the Top Fifty. Frankly I'm not really bothered about it. The whole Loder inspired Crass financial world was a mystery to most, including many members of Crass, but I wasn't doing it for the money. That was why I had been so keen on the free gig scene. Money sullies everything. Even something as seemingly pure as Crass. Plus I was under no illusions about why our record sold so well anyway. It wasn't because the name Zounds was on the label, it was because of the reputation of Crass.

The thing that wasn't fun about the whole saga was Penny and Loder's insistence that we use a session drummer. They didn't think Joseph could keep time. Maybe he couldn't, but then neither could I. To me it reeked of music-biz sell out, and this from the kings of anarchist rock. Joseph was crest-fallen. I was uncomfortable and tried to console myself with the knowledge that it was standard music-biz practice, and that everyone from the Beatles on down had session drummers on their first record. But wasn't this supposed to be different? Wasn't this the punk revolution of honesty, integrity and making what you could out of your own idiosyncratic and limited talents? Joseph never complained and never showed any resentment about it, but I thought it was crap. Crass were into high production values, and I know they had reasons for that. But even serial killers justify what they do. Penny explained that the whole hippie thing had failed because it was essentially weak and flimsy, passive and amateurish. If any new social movement was to have any chance of success then it had to be strong, confident and active. It had to demonstrate it could create work that was as professional and well produced as anything else. It had to prove that it could compete with capitalist, mainstream products. I didn't agree, in fact I thought that logic was a little bit patriarchal. Showing 'the men' that you could play them at 'the man's game'. I thought we needed a new game, an alternative society, not just a replication of old ways and old values. The guy Penny hired was a great drummer and it made it a better record, that is undeniable, but it wasn't the way it was supposed to be, it left a nasty taste in the mouth.

It took ages to do the vocals, I got through most of the song relatively painlessly, but then spent well over three hours trying to get the last line of the song exactly as Penny wanted it. I just did it over and over and over again. Joseph and Laurence were losing the will to live in the control room. I'm not sure the last version was any better or any different to the first, but at last Penny was satisfied and it was in the can.

The next time we saw him they had mixed the record, designed the cover, written the sleeve notes and had it in production. I don't remember ever being consulted about anything. It was a bit like being on Tamla Motown or Stock, Aitkin and Waterman in a way. They chose the songs, produced the record, designed the image and controlled every part of the process. I'm not complaining about any of this though, it was the Crass label and they weren't forcing us to be on it.

Music lyrics structure

Can't Cheat Karma is the second song I wrote for Zounds and is the oldest in the Zounds repertoire. It is a weird song with a weird structure. I actually came up with the main part of the song as I was walking down the Cowley Road in Oxford sometime in 1977. I wanted to do one of those Frank Zappa type things where you get a line of singing and then a riff. The riff was pretty mundane the way I conceived it, but Steve Burch (the original guitar player) found a way of phrasing it that kicked the whole thing into a fierier domain altogether. No one else ever managed to play it with the same commitment, passion and force that Steve did, even the record is a pale imitation.

It remains one of Zounds most popular songs. That is also weird for me because I have always regarded it as something of a failure. I thought it had some good lyrical ideas, but they are thrown away and artlessly executed. It was a longer song originally with a slow section at the beginning full of clichéd nonsense about big business, we dropped that quite quickly! I guess it is one of those confessional songs that were a mainstay of a particular punk sensibility at that time. I suppose what I am trying to say is, 'let's cut the crap and be honest here, I am a pathetic ego-maniac, a shallow, self obsessed show off, a liar and a wanker, and no one else is any better.' I think it is probably a pretty accurate picture of myself as a person absolutely alienated and confused by what was going on in the world, who I was, what my place was and where I was going. Nothing's changed much really.

Peace has gotta come but I just got hate

One of our ex-guitarists had come up with the odd instrumental section in the middle of the song. We never credited him on the record. We never actually credited anybody as composer on the record, we just said it was by Zounds. But let's be clear about this, I fucking wrote the fucking song. I heard from a mutual friend that the ex-guitarist felt the band had become successful on the back of his middle eight! Ironically we always thought the middle section was a bit weak and wimpy and we dropped it from live performances of the song almost as soon as the record was finished, we still just do the verses and choruses, and he still hates me apparently.

Ultimately I thought the song was a promising start with a few good lines but it never really added up for me.

02 WAR

War in Afghanistan
War in Northern Ireland
War in South America
War in Africa

War - Violence
War - Oppression

Violence in London
Violence in Bristol
Violence in New York
Violence in Moscow

War - Violence
War - Oppression

War in Heaven
Unrest on Earth
War in my head
War in my house

War - War - War - War

War

★

'War . What is it good for – absolutely nothing - say it again'

Sadly this song never dates. The locations change, the conflicts are different, but it is always there, in actuality and in threat. It is always there in people's heads. While there is war in people's heads there will be war on earth (and one day maybe beyond). The impetus to war is there in family arguments, in neighbourhood rivalries, in the relationships of lovers. It is present in the relationship between the people and the state. War is the ultimate expression of conflict, violence taken to its extreme. While there is violence in the minds of people there will be war.

War moves into every area of life. Now it's on the Internet, servers are attacking each other. When the Internet started it seemed like this great semi-anarchic free space for the exchange of audio, video, text, images, ideas and everything else. Now it has become a vast network, policed by States for and on behalf of global corporate interests. Big money belies the myth of big society.

There is no war without warriors. There are no leaders without followers. No one to lead you into war if you will not follow them. I don't believe there is such a thing as a war crime, war is a crime. Reformed wife beater John Lennon once made the glib pronouncement that 'war is over if you want it'. He was right, it's deep in the psych and will endure until we no longer want it or have it in us.

I always told people I was homeless when I wrote this. My memory tells me that my friend Ricky and I went up to Shepherd's Bush in London, to stay with his dad for a few days. Ricky was really into Reggae, as most people were in those days. We spent a couple of days listening to the 1977 'Live At The Rainbow' album by the Wailers. It contained the Bob Marley song 'War', based on a speech by Haile Selassie 1. After constant listening I wrote my own song called War. Thinking back on it, the timing doesn't add up though, so I must have made that up and started believing it. In fact this whole thing could be a tissue of confused half-truths, sub-conscious lies and dope smokers false memory syndrome.

03 SUBVERT

If you gotta job
You can be an agent
You can work for revolution
In your place of employment
If you gotta job you can be an agent
You can work for revolution in your place of employment
Employed in a factory throw a spanner in the works
Internal sabotage, hits them where it hurts

Subvert - Subvert - Subvert - Subvert

If you gotta job
Where they treat you like a slave
Where they treat you like a zombie
In their corporate grave
If you work in an office making tea for the bosses
They are getting richer on ten time your pay
They may think you're stupid but you're working
undercover
You've got the potential to disobey

Subvert - Subvert - Subvert - Subvert

If you've got a job
Cos there's nothing else to do
Where they think they've got you trapped in
The boxes that they choose
If you've got a job you can be an agent
If you work in a kitchen you can redistribute food
If you are a policeman ordered to arrest me
You don't have to do it, you can refuse

Subvert - Subvert - Subvert - Subvert

School - army - work - play

As a child in England during the 1960s, when you reached the age of eleven, you were required to take an exam that would determine the type of school you would go to from then on. The type of school you went to decided the type of future you would have. Some kids didn't need to take the exam because they were from rich families who would pay for them to have private education. These children would go on to become the leaders of industry, army, government, church and anything else that needed leaders.

If you passed the exam you went to a 'grammar school'. Here you were prepared for a future as a white-collar manager, a junior executive, a low to middle ranking officer in the armed forces, a doctor or an architect.

If you failed the exam you went to something called a 'Secondary Modern'. These prepared you for a life in the lower orders, something akin to the 'Epsilons' in Aldous Huxley's Brave New World.

Secondary Moderns turned out the army privates who would become cannon fodder in the war zones of the world. They also produced the unskilled factory drones that would work the tedious production lines, and the manual labourers who would break their backs in under-valued, low paid, monotonous hard graft.

I wasn't very bright and I came from a working class family. I failed the 11 Plus exam and ended up in Maiden Erlegh Secondary Modern School. Despite ambitions to become an actor, my real destiny was fulfilled, and at the age of sixteen I became a factory drone. I had one career interview at school where they asked me if I would consider joining the army. I told them I had considered it and it was the last thing on earth I would do. My classmate David Atwood joined up. I advised him against it, but I didn't hate him for it.

I am a bit ambivalent about people that do join up. Whilst being inclined against the waging of war and violent behaviour of any kind, I understand why kids like my friend do it. They've been brought up on a media and cultural diet of war-glorification, adventure, righteousness, excitement and fun. It's that or the factory. Or its modern day equivalent, i.e. being a low status phone monkey in an anonymous call centre. Acting as the mouthpiece for some faceless, cock-sucking, corporate monster that will sap your will, your imagination, your time and your energy. It's fucking boring and the pay's crap.

So while my friend went off to the army, I worked in factories, warehouses, kitchens and building sites all over East Berkshire. Places like Gillette's, Courage Breweries, Marconi Weapons Systems, Parker Timber, Waitrose, ICL, IBM. I did every lowly job imaginable and built up a lot of resentment in the process. I was crushed, really crushed. That sort of work didn't suit me. I had imagination even if I had no ambition. These soul-destroying places were grim and joyless and boring in the extreme. School had been bad enough, but this was much, much worse, and it would go on forever. I hated it. Of course there were moments when you would have fun with all your other epsilon mates (and a few students and wastrels who were either slumming it, filling in time, or had completely failed to live up to their parents' expectations). But on the whole the good times revolved around 'goofing off', and little acts of unfocused, intuitive subversion and revenge. Little pointless things that did nothing to change the overall scheme of things, but would at least give you the sense that you could have one or two little victories at the expense of the distant bosses.

Despite the grandiose claims of the lyric, 'Subvert' was more about those little acts of personal and group sabotage than it was about any real revolutionary act. Frankly I knew fuck all about revolution, fuck all about politics and fuck all about much else. All I knew was that the television had promised me and my type a shiny, silver-foil suited, space-age future where robots would do all the work, computers would solve all our problems, energy would be almost free, and our only dilemma would be what to do with all our leisure time. Instead we ended up shovelling shit with no prospect of improvement. I was seriously pissed off about the whole deal

Right to work (right to call in sick in the head)

When we were teenage doleys and factory fodder kicking around

Reading in the early 1970s, we would often see the slogans 'right to work' or 'fight for the right to work' graffitied round the town. For all I know these slogans probably date back to the 1930s. They still get trotted out today. Presumably daubed up by some witless, unimaginative left wing group whose minds are as wedded to wage-slavery as their capitalist masters. The idea that I would expend energy trying to fight for the right to get up too early, spend all day involved in some relentless, repetitive, mind numbing task, and then be too knackered to do anything other than drink myself into a stupor or watch endless hours of crummy TV was frankly absurd.

I was always suspicious of the left after that. Often it seems like they are on your side, but in the final analysis they are as keen on authoritarian, hierarchical, meritocratic systems as any one else. Their romanticised idea of the dignity of industrialised labour is simultaneously laughable and sad. I mean, if you want to work in a brick factory, sweating in the heat of the furnaces, breaking your back, straining your eyes and breathing in thick dust until your lungs seize up, go ahead. It's just that I don't. It's too dark and noisy (but not in a good way). It happened to my grandfather and I wasn't about to let it happen to me.

My attitude to work is pretty much summed up by the anarchist/anti-anarchist writer and thinker Bob Black. Though I don't know him so I am not associating myself with any of his other ideas. He talks about the abolition of work as we know it, and replacing it with productive play. He concludes:

"Life will become a game, or rather many games, but not — as it is now—a zero/sum game. An optimal sexual encounter is the paradigm of productive play. The participants potentiate each other's pleasures, nobody keeps score, and everybody wins. The more you give, the more you get. In the lucid life, the best of sex will diffuse into the better part of daily life. Generalized play leads to the libidinization of life. Sex, in turn, can become less urgent and desperate, more playful. If we play our cards right, we can all get more out of life than we put into it; but only if we play for keeps."

BOB BLACK

Rough Trade and the Curse of Zounds

*Sacked By Crass - Rough Trade - Boy George's Lover -
Socialist Millionaire Record Producers -
Jamaican Mixers - Cliff Harper And The Cover Art*

Sacked by Crass

The first single came out and rocketed to number one in the Indie charts (through no fault of our own). We went over to Dial House to meet with Crass. Laurence didn't turn up, his squat had been raided and he was arrested for 'obstructing the police in the course of their duty'. His obstruction turned out to be grabbing a lump of hash and swallowing it in order to escape a possession charge, as the police burst though the door. At Dial House Penny was very excited about the way the record had turned out and the reaction to it, and suggested we do an album for Crass, with him again in the producer's chair. We even spoke about the title and the cover.

Once we felt ready to record we went back over to Dial House to arrange a schedule, but the mood had changed and it all seemed a bit awkward. Penny started to explain that Crass didn't want to function as a conventional record label. Gee interrupted and told us they had no interest in other people's music. While they were willing to give bands a hand by releasing one-off records, they were not interested in developing anyone's career, and did not want to get involved in the day to day minutiae of bringing out and promoting other band's records. This would have come as news to the Poison Girls who made three singles and two albums for Crass, and had even received cash advances from them in order to buy their house in Leyton.

I didn't mind about it and I wasn't surprised by their lack of interest in other people's music either. They made it quite clear they were not even interested in their own music. To them, music was just a vehicle to get their message across. They were an ideological, propaganda machine who used music and art as a medium to propagate their ideas, whereas Zounds were fully fledged, immature, rock n roll children who lived to play gigs, loved Elvis and Hank Williams, and just happened to write songs about their lives as disaffected squatters with no ambition. I think it was only Steve Ignorant who genuinely liked Crass' music. Without him they would have just been another bunch of middle-class, art terrorists. Steve lent them an authenticity and a genuine 'voice of the streets'. I mean, let's face it, most of the people in Crass came from places that were so posh they didn't even have streets.

It's possible I'm doing Penny a disservice. He always seemed genuinely excited about his production work. He would talk enthusiastically about Poison Girls being The Jefferson Airplane of psychedelic punk, and how he had applied bells and gongs and slowed down vocals to things like The Mob's 'No Doves Fly Here', or their own 'Nagasaki Nightmare'. I think Penny would have liked to have done more with Zounds, but on this very rare occasion was vetoed by other factions in the camp.

Goodbye anarchists, hello Marxists

Being cast out of the bosom of the Crass collective, we were at a loss to know what to do next. I suggested we go down to Rough Trade and see if we could meet Geoff Travis and ask him what to do. The three of us trolled over to West London and went to the Rough Trade warehouse and announced that we were Zounds and that we wanted to talk to Geoff Travis. Out came Geoff who was immediately friendly and open. 'Hi boys, absolutely love the record, sorry I haven't been to see you live yet. How can I help?' I explained the Crass situation and he said 'how would you like to record for Rough Trade? You could do an album and another single. How do you see it sounding?'
At which point Joseph said 'Like the Dead Kennedys'. Which was news to me.
'Shall we go into my office and look at some recording dates? You should do it at Berry Street with Adam Kidron engineering'.

I was completely blown away by this. It was like a cheesy Hollywood film, it all just seemed too easy. It was one thing being on Crass records with a load of other weirdos, but suddenly Zounds, the most untrendy band in the world, were being asked on to the hippest record label of the era. Maybe Geoff thought we were a different band altogether. I always found him very fair, very friendly and very supportive. When Rough Trade was going through some financial difficulties Geoff financed 'More Trouble' with his personal money. The only reason they were in difficulty was because of the shoddy way the banks dealt with them, due to the fact Rough Trade was a worker's co-operative.

As groovy as Rough Trade was, I never really felt a part of it. Geoff and Peter Walmsley, and one or two others, were really great, but the staff were intimidating with their trendy haircuts and hipper-than-thou demeanour. Rough Trade never really knew what to do with us. We didn't actually fit in to the neo-Marxist, art-student niche many of their bands subscribed too. We met Green of Scritti Pollitti and one or two others. They seemed fine, but while they were engaged with the complex and sophisticated ideas of Jacques Derrida and Michel Foucault, we liked the Fabulous Furry Freak Brothers and The Beano.

The Rough Trade Agency tried to get us gigs, but they were always in trendy clubs where no one was interested and most of our audience couldn't get in because of age and licensing restrictions. The worst thing they booked us on to was a national tour supporting Mick Jones protégées Theatre Of Hate. At the first gig in Gillingham 'the Hate' paraded around, pouting and preening and acting like wannabe rock stars. Of course their absence of talent, half-baked ideas and lack of personality meant they would never be able to achieve that goal. They spent a lot of time combing and teasing their hair, applying make up and posing in front of mirrors. To little avail, they still looked like knob-heads. We of course kept ourselves to ourselves and smoked dope, chatted shit and told jokes. When 'the Hate' saw that not only did we have dope, but we were also accompanied by our own personal, in-house dealer, they hassled us to give them drugs. We were surprised as in the press they purported to have a strong anti-drugs stance. But then nothing about them was real. Their singer even tried, unsuccessfully, to sue Boy George when George wrote about their love affair in his autobiography. The singer pretended he wasn't gay, but at that time you could see them together any Thursday night up at Islington's Pied Bull, the way they kissed and held hands and cavorted together certainly looked gay. Don't know what 'the Boy' saw in him really. I always thought George seemed like quite a nice, genuine person. No accounting for bad taste though.

The next date on the ill-fated tour was a ballroom in Southampton.

'Theatre of Stupid' got really pissed off then. We seemed to have more fans in the hall than them and that really shattered their fragile, over-developed egos. It was probably the reason it all blew up the next night at Nottingham University. They did a mind-numbingly long sound check. On and on it went with their overblown, symphonic drums echoing round and round the hall. It left us very little time to set up and do our own preparations. When we did finally clamber up on the boards, our bill-topping buffoons started using the P.A. to play back tapes of the tedious sound-check they had just done. We asked what the fuck was going on and they claimed that, as we had so far not paid the £25 a night for the P.A. hire, we couldn't use it for the rest of the tour. Well, no one had told us we were supposed to pay to play, and nobody had offered us any payment. Rough Trade had booked the gigs and had presumably agreed to pay hire charges and collect fees for us. I didn't fucking know, and was frankly not interested. I just wanted to play my songs. In all my life I have never come across a more petulant bunch of tossers. We told them they were at liberty to insert their P.A. where the sun doesn't shine and we walked off the tour. It is wankers like these that make me feel embarrassed to be part of the whole rock music circus. Give me Jerry Lee Lewis any day.

Those music-biz gigs and games never really worked out for Zounds. Out of all the trendy bands we played with, the only pleasant ones turned out to be The Birthday Party. Nice polite lads who were sociable, unpretentious and approachable. At least they didn't pretend not to take drugs, and Nick Cave even helped me carry my bass cab from the street to the stage, quite a nice geezer for a 'dark lord of Goth'.

The curse of Adam Kidron

We recorded the Curse Of Zounds plus both sides of the Demystification single in four days and mixed it in less than two. The engineer was Adam Kidron. He was the son of a socialist millionaire publisher who owned Pluto Press. Adam's sister, Biba Kidron, would go on to make the influential agitprop film 'Carry Greenham Home'; later still she would direct the less influential 'Bridget Jones: The Edge Of Reason'. Adam was certainly moving in ritzier circles than the decidedly un-well connected Zounds. He was a highly charismatic and entertaining individual who was simultaneously working with Scritti Politti, Wah Heat and many other Rough Trade related acts. His two favourite places were Moscow and Los Angeles, and he'd given up doing Maths at Oxford to become a record producer. We were captivated by him. But then, we were completely stoned out of our gourds the whole time and easily impressed. He also said he hated guitars and only liked soul and jazz. Gulp! We were all about guitars. One late night when we were particularly out of it Adam whispered to us conspiratorially, 'I usually get a producer's credit and four points on anything I work on, is that OK?' Naïf's that we were, we had no idea what points were, and had no problem with him getting a production credit. 'Yea, fine' we capitulated. 'Great, I'll tell Geoff you've agreed it' he replied, going back to making some vital adjustments at the mixing desk. It turned out points were a percentage of the royalties, so we were done up like a kipper there. It was great fun working with him, but as with the Crass recordings the guitars were not big enough, and mixed too quietly.

All the way from Kingston Jamaica

It was always difficult with engineers and producers. Geoff got Mickey Dread in to produce 'Dancing' and 'True Love'. Mickey was a Jamaican D.J. and producer of some repute and was in England producing and recording with The Clash for their 'Sandinista' album. His work with us was somewhat less successful, but then we had no pretensions to play reggae, and unlike Joe Strummer and Mick Jones, did not wish we had been born in a 'government yard in Trench Town'.

Mickey didn't actually turn up for any of the recording. We gathered in the studio and waited. He called to say he was delayed and we should get started without him, he would pick up the reins when he arrived. He assured us he would be there in an hour. We got started and the hours drifted by. He called again. He had been further delayed but would be there in an hour. This went on for the whole of the two days of recording. Another day was booked for the mix and he did actually manage to get there for that and even contribute a couple of ideas. He had a very strong Jamaican accent that I found impenetrable most of the time. Though strangely, when the subject of 'points' reared it's ugly head again, he was perfectly clear and comprehensible, and made himself understood very easily.

Cliff Harper

When it came to the cover art for The Curse Of Zounds I wanted to use a Cliff Harper illustration that he had done for the cover of Anarchy Magazine during a Fire Fighter's strike. I just wanted to use it in a fanzine style and stick it on a bit of paper. But Cliff asked to redraw it. Such a lovely simple idea, which he claimed was more or less, copied from a Jak cartoon in the Evening Standard, quite a right wing paper. Classic example of how context affects the way you read an image. We got him £30 from Rough Trade and he redrew it beautifully, coming up with a powerful and iconic image. I sometimes think I prefer the cover to the album.

04 DEMYSTIFICATION

I look out the window and I wonder at it all,
Staring at the symbols that decorate the wall,
Everybody's calling to come and join them all,
But I can't go with no one till I understand the call.

Don't come round for me unless you've got what I,
Don't come round for me unless you've got what I,
Don't come round for me unless you've got what I want.
I want some demystification,
I want some demystification,
I want some demystification about what's going on.

My electronic shaver won't plug into the wall,
Now I can't go to the party the electrician didn't call,
And I hear they're counting numbers to store down in
Whitehall,
So much information what can they do with it all?

Don't come round for me unless you've got what I,
Don't come round for me unless you've got what I,
Don't come round for me unless you've got what I want.
I want some demystification,
I want some demystification,
I want some demystification about what's going on.

Some people talk of Shiva and some they talk of God,
Some talk of politicians and some they talk of love,
They mystify their heroes offer chances we could take,
I'm not looking for escapism I just want to escape.

Demystification

*Banned by Rough Trade - Songwriting - E minor - Drones -
Pop - Graffiti in Brougham Road - Religion - Zen And The Art
of Motorcycle Maintenance - No such thing as originality*

Banned by Rough Trade - Thatcher's tits

Dr. Inadequate Phuck (a.k.a Richard Chubb, a.k.a. Gubby) had drawn the strange soldier/wolf poster included with the first single. Never was totally sure what the relevance was, but we liked Gubby's slightly 'Crumb-esque' drawing, and we were always keen to allow our friends a platform. We asked him to do a cover for Demystification. He came up with an image of Margaret Thatcher as a many armed Indian God, surrounded by various agents of the State, portrayed as her acolytes. In the way of some Indian gods Thatcher was bare breasted. We took the cover to Geoff Travis, one of the few nice people in the music industry. He promptly told us Rough Trade couldn't release the record in such a sleeve. He said he couldn't justify it to his feminist friends and that he himself was uncomfortable with portraying women naked.

We were bemused as the drawing was a caricature, and in no way sexualised. Obviously we would never knowingly have used any image that might contribute to the commodification of female sexuality. But I never considered nakedness in itself to be wrong. Christian, bourgeois society has made sex dirty, and the body taboo. Under various post-pagan religious doctrines, sex became privatised and secret. It became a source of repression and shame. My feeling was that this was part of the reason why sex had become fetishised and industrialised. My somewhat unoriginal view was: the hang-ups that come from religious sexual repression and body-fear fuel the sex industry, violence against women, prostitution and the associated physical and psychological horrors that accompany those things. Zounds could never be part of that. Although we didn't agree with Geoff that this could be construed as a sexist image, we consented to the 'self-censorship'.

Anyway, we were learning all the time, and never felt like we had all the answers. It was a time of exploring all the conventional power relationships in our own lives, especially those between men and women. Obviously representation of gender was one of the key facets. These were matters that were being worked out in our homes and lives all the time. Rock groups usually inhabit a very male oriented space, in an atmosphere that can easily regress into macho posturing. But we weren't living in that kind of rock n roll world, and didn't particularly want to. We were in squats and communities where strong, independent women often took the lead in social, intellectual, political and artistic activity. There were many separatist and lesbian women's houses round Brougham Road, Broadway Market and London Fields. The women Zounds were sharing their lives with constantly challenged us. A number of London Fields women were Spanish and steeped in the history and ideas of anarchist, syndicalist and feminist thought. Most of the men in our scene were not only educated about sexism by women, but also about sex itself. But that's another story.

Of course, we had a long way to go in the consciousness raising stakes and it is not always easy to purge bourgeois conditioning. But at least we were trying. The explosion of Punk rock gave us all a chance to reinvent and remake ourselves, both men and women. In her film 'Women in Punk' Zillah Minx says

"Punk gave women a chance to really explore who they wanted to be".

That was very liberating for men as well as women. Women's liberation always seemed quite threatening to some men, but you can't be free when you're bound to slaves. Therefore the liberation of women must surely lead to the liberation of men. The questioning of women's roles by women meant men could question their own place in the set up. It freed men to explore aspects of their personalities that didn't conform to the heroic, macho, 'real-man' of mainstream representation. It also allowed some men to come out as homosexuals without the threat of violence and psychological abuse. Well they could in Brougham Road and the Angel Housing Co-op anyway.

The censorship of the Demystification cover wasn't a question of being 'right on' or 'politically correct' ('ideologically sound' as we would have said at the time). It was a question of having some integrity, and trying to build a better world that was not based on ignorance. Sadly banning the cover did not turn back the tide. As I write, highly sexualised images of women grinding and gyrating in nothing but leather thongs and tit-tassels are used to advertise every thing from cars and football to gardening equipment and grouting. Some people claim that this and the rise of pole dancing and other dubious arts are a measure of the confidence and liberation of the modern woman. I don't know and it's not for me to say. I still take the old fashioned view that they are complicit in their own oppression, but then, aren't we all.

I mourn the fact that the women's movement has so far been unable to change the behaviour of men significantly. It might be that men should change themselves, but left to their own devices I don't think men can change. Someone needs to give them a lead and a helping hand if they are to replace values based on aggression. (Come on girls – pull your finger out!)

It's not about sex, it's about sexism, and it is about power. Some individual women might do very well out of the way things are, but it sets the scene and sets the agenda for so many other male/female interactions, which still don't seem that healthy to me.

Penny Rimbaud said we should have brought the picture of the bare breasted Thatcher to Crass and they would have covered up the offending bosom. He was also a bit disappointed we didn't put the lyrics on the cover. I think that was the last time I went out to Dial House.

Still worrying after all these years

It took me a while to track down a copy of the Thatcher drawing for this book, and when I did I realised there was a whole other issue that we all completely missed at the time. Which in itself demonstrates how far we still had to go in terms of consciousness raising. That was the use of the word 'retarded' in Gubby's signature. Like many of us, Gubby was quite damaged and quite vulnerable. As a result he often resorted to self-deprecation. Why else would he choose the pen name Dr. Inadequate Phuck? As a satirist he parodied the affectation of academics who ornament their names with strings of initials signifying their qualifications. Following Gubby's signature we see the letters 'G.B.H. and 'L.S.D. We also see the word 'retarded', used as a pun on 'retired', aping the crusty old colonels who would write to the Times complaining about the incorrect use of the apostrophe, the loss of the British empire, and demanding flogging for homosexuals.

The casual use of the 'vocabulary of madness' is of course as important as sexism and racism in language and image. Representation of disability and mental and physical illness were not as present on our radar then. Prejudice and discrimination are all contained within the casual and derogatory terms we use to refer to disability and illness, just as they are with sexism and racism. I don't give a fuck about what people consider 'politically correct' or 'ideologically sound'. I am also happy to offend people if I want to, in fact sometimes it is necessary. But I have no intention of hurting anyone if I can help it. The world can be a cruel, damaging and bewildering place, and I take no pleasure in adding to that. I am sure I do all the time, but I don't mean to.

Song writing

I have strong memories of writing this song in my bedroom at 64 Brougham Road, Hackney. There are many ways to write a song and I use a variety of methods. This time though I did the classic (probably most common) songwriter thing of sitting down fiddling with the guitar and coming up with the basic chord sequence. Like a lot of my songs it is based around Em, C and D. I always feel the guitar is designed for the key of E minor. It's the easiest chord to play and booms out, all the strings ringing, and you can move the shape up and down and get nice, slightly dissonant chords that are atmospheric and droney. You get the whole body of the instrument, as most of the strings are open. Laurence and I really liked chord sequences that had droning strings that didn't change throughout a sequence, always part of the appeal of the Velvet Underground for me.

One of the attractive things about droney music is that you can hear different things in it every time you listen. It offers up a world of possibilities as the notes and overtones clash and interact. Different note combinations jump out at you, particularly when it is on the edge of dissonance. While writing Demystification I played on that effect by moving the E minor shape up to the 9th and 10th frets and repeating it. Looking for somewhere to go next I did what I always do in my musically unsophisticated way, I tried going to C and D. Immediately I had that interesting contrast between the droney, atmospheric bit and the more poppy C – D progression.

43

I don't think I was trying to write about anything in particular at that moment. I was just trying to write. Finding something to write about is often a problem.

Sometimes you feel like you've got something to say, sometimes you don't. Most of the time I felt (and feel) like I've got nothing worthwhile to say. So there I was strumming and humming, developing the melody and looking out of the window at the graffiti strewn, corrugated iron fence that separated the squats from the building site on the opposite side of the road. The graffiti was a collection of political slogans and symbols and random nonsense. So lazily I just started describing the scene. Once you get a couple of lines it can happen that the rest of it just pours out from the sub-conscious. You don't always know what it is you are doing. Presumably the idea that 'things are made mysterious and impenetrable as a way of disempowering and controlling people' worked its way to the forefront of my mind. I just ploughed on and out it came, and I can trace where every line comes from.

There are ideas I encountered in the novel 'Zen And The Art Of Motorcycle Maintenance'. Not a particularly good book, but it was the first time I encountered the notion that people are trapped by a lack of understanding regarding the physical processes of life. How the inability to understand the physical world can lead to impotence. The electronic shaver doesn't work, you can't make yourself look nice, so you don't go out. Not that any of us ever bothered about being presentable. But I often wrote from the perspective of the 'ordinary Joe', not the perspective of a load of disaffected, bohemian, anti-establishment, dope smoking, soap dodgers, which is what we were.

Some of the lyrics refer directly to something Debby Webb told me about the government collecting statistical information about men, in order to re-introduce military conscription. I don't think it was true but it is a sign of the times that we were prepared to believe it.

Other lines refer to an anarchist/atheist poster Debby had at her house. This contained the lines 'why look for escapism when you can really escape'. Such a great line, I just had to steal it for the song.

Song writing for me is often a case of collecting/nicking ideas from other contexts and putting them in songs. This is a common strategy for most songwriters. Actually, a lot of times it just involves taking ideas from one song and putting them into another. That's one of the reasons I'm not that bothered about copyright. The ideas come out of the air and the music is developed within the culture. If you write a blues or a country song how can you claim you have come up with that harmonic sequence. Even in jazz they mostly use standard 32 bar progressions, you can put your own twist on it, but you didn't invent it. And the same with lyrics. Ideas are in the culture, you might make them rhyme and set them to a tune, but they are rarely your original idea.

Julian Cope once said 'don't be original'. He claims that everything he does has been done before. I don't think there is any choice in it, not in rock music anyway. Anything you do, someone has done (usually better).

05 GREAT WHITE HUNTER

I am the Great White Hunter
And you know I've come to search
Just to further human knowledge
All for science and research

And if by chance I bring back
What I am looking for
They'll be someone somewhere waiting
With their fingers round a purse

I am the missionary Christian
I'm taking bibles to the blacks
I am spreading western culture
And I'm collecting all the tax

I'm taking whiskey to the natives
Tribal carvings to Chelsea
Because a market's just a market
Working for the bourgeoisie

But don't associate me with that no more
I may be the same colour but I am sure
I'm not like that and I never will
Condone the things they do and the reasons that they kill

Well I will murder baby seals
And I'll sell their skins for gold
I'll murder Indians in the jungle
Just to make way for a road

And I will fight guerrilla armies
All for profit, not for cause
I'll sell arms to rival armies
And make profit from their wars

I am the Great White Hunter
I am the great exploiter
I am the great destroyer
I am the Great White Hunter

Great White Hunter

'Some V.U. white light returned with thanks'

Guilt - inner cities and the third world - the country and the city

Joseph always described this as The Velvet Underground meets white liberal guilt. Velvet Underground? I wish. Guilt? I don't know about that. I never felt a part of things enough to feel the guilt of association. No one was going to war, clubbing seals and polluting the oceans on my say so.

To me it just seemed that those who were profiting from capitalism were exploiting the working classes of the west in the same way they exploited everything else, unfeelingly, dispassionately and effectively. They are the 'Great White Hunters', not me. The British working class had always been victims of the same system that violently colonised the world. The mines, mills and factories of England's industrial towns were as horrific a part of the colonial economy as the conquered lands overseas. Consider, the average age of mortality of Wool combers in West Bradford in 1844 was seventeen, in East Bradford it was only fourteen!

In the early 1980s there were people who proposed the idea that British inner-cities were part of the third-world. I don't know if that was true because I'd only ever seen the third world on television, but it certainly seemed that way in Hackney where we were living. And places like it, Lambeth, Tower Hamlets and other great swathes of London. It was no different in St Pauls in Bristol, Handsworth in Birmingham, Toxteth in Liverpool. These places were desolate and bleak, perfectly and chillingly evoked in The Specials song 'Ghost Town', and the Mike Leigh film 'Mean Time'. Grim, deteriorating places with poor housing, high unemployment, few amenities and people on the bread line competing for low pay, low status jobs, and with no way out.

The 'political right' in Britain has a long history of divide and rule, from the Conservative Party to the National Front and the

British National Party. They have all tried to inflame and separate communities along the lines of race and nationality. But always it is economic and cultural class issues that are the real divider. Blame for economic hardship is often based on the demonising of the 'immigrant'. But everyone in the inner city was/is an immigrant, or the descendant of an immigrant. Not just from former overseas colonies scattered throughout the West Indies, Africa, Asia or wherever. But also those that stumbled, limped and drifted in from the British countryside and small rural towns. Agricultural workers and rural dwellers who couldn't make a living off the land, crafts people looking for places to sell their wares and services. People thrown off the land by enclosures, clearances and the industrialisation of agriculture and intensive land management. Bored young people escaping the uniformity of suburban dormitory towns. The mashing up of all these people who meet, interact and exchange experiences and outlooks is one of the particularly exciting things about London.

For a while, everyone I knew in London, came from somewhere else. It was a bit of a surprise when, after a while, I started to meet people that had been born in London. I thought of them as oddities and slightly exotic. There is still an aspect of London that is like a cowboy town full of displaced hill farmers. London is a big place for music, but the bands tend to go there rather than come from there, disproportionately when you consider its size.

It is easy to forget that cities evolve simply by loads of people banding together for work, company, safety, fun, excitement or circumstance. Cities don't just spring up fully formed and fully populated. They constantly regenerate and renew. The populations are fluid. No one owns the cities, they are just there for whoever is in them at the time. That's why they are so brilliant and sometimes frightening, though not as frightening as the countryside can be. I'm sure if I spent much time out there I would be the first to be trussed up in a Wicker Man and sacrificed by ferociously insular pagans, for unspecified crimes against some local, idiosyncratic custom. Which in itself is likely based on an irrational belief in some hallucinatory, unseen, minor deity.

I don't feel comfortable in places where everyone knows everything about you; places where if you get on the wrong side of someone, you have to see them and their family every day. Where a few powerful residents form little oligarchies to control the local economy. Where ordinary people know their place, doff their caps and defer to their betters. Small places where suspicion and petty-xenophobia alienates and discriminates against outsiders, anything, or anyone, that is different or unusual. Places where the phrase 'are you local' seems to carry the whiff of malice and violence. It's something that worries me about the localism and small community bias of the eco-movement. You sometimes get a whiff of it at folk festivals. A weird alliance of latter day hippies, crossed with the 'countryside alliance', and fermented in an atmosphere of proud traditionalism, petty-nationalism and witchy new-ageism.

The countryside is a nice place to go for a walk though!

06 FEAR

Sing a song of violence and listen for the sound
All the little soldiers start to come around
Start it with a rumour, a whisper in an ear
Suspicion don't take very long before it turns to fear
They don't need a reason, they don't want to know
Who or what they're fighting, just tell them where to go
Give the chance of glory, give the chance of fame
Give the boy an enemy, give the dog a name
Keep the factions fighting, start them off at school
Keep the factions fighting so you divide and rule
Football teams are splendid and fashion just a tool
Keep the factions fighting so you divide and rule

Fear can be a bum thing
A silly and a dumb thing
Fear can be the one thing
That keeps us all apart
Fear can be a bum thing
A silly and a dumb thing
Fear can be the one thing
That keeps us in the dark

Frightened of the humans and frightened of their stares
Frightened of the poisons they pump into the air
Frightened of the chemicals they spray upon the land
Frightened of the power they hold within their hands
Frightened of bureaucracy and frightened of the law
Frightened of the government and who it's working for
Frightened of the children who won't know how to cope
With a world in rack and ruin from their technocratic
dope, dope, dope

Fear

Family - Church – State - Police - Nuclear power - Mutually assured destruction - No wonder you're edgy

Some people walk around in those t-shirts that say 'no fear'. Not me. My life is ruled by fear. I have lived with fear as a constant companion since the beginning of my conscious life (and probably before).

I was scared of everything, even my own shadow. I was scared of being alone with the big, ugly crucifix and rosary on the wall next to my bedroom. I was terrified of Father Collins, the rather traditional, Irish Catholic Priest who would visit our home to 'administer the fear of god' and preside over our religious well-being. I was frightened by my bipolar mother and her violent temper that could express itself in ferocious physical attacks on me. I was scared witless by the horrific fights between my mother and father, which would sometimes see my sister and I cowering under the table as mum attacked dad with carving knives and bottles. I was nervous of strangers. When I discovered illness I became frightened of that. Other kids, dogs, teachers, the police, being alone, being abandoned, getting lost, the water, pretty much everything I encountered had the potential to induce terror.

Once, when I was about three or four years old, I ran excitedly out of our house onto the street. As I turned out of the gate, an ugly, snarling council worker in dark blue overalls was scything the grass verge. I stopped dead in my tracks, he caught sight of me and let out a blood-curdling growl and waved his scythe menacingly at me. I leapt back in shock and terror and ran blubbering back into the house.

Another time, some of the older kids persuaded the toddlers on the estate to go ditch jumping with them. The ditch was actually a small brook with water a couple of feet deep. Unfortunately I leapt but didn't make it to the other side. I plunged straight into the middle of the brook and fell down into the mud and the slime and the water. I managed to scramble out, soaked from head to toe and probably resembling some filthy, Dickensian, mud lark. I ran home to my mother, shivering and crying. Instead of the love and comfort I so badly needed, she shouted and beat me. I was crying even harder. Crying, always crying.

At night I had recurring nightmares involving wolves and the crucifix. Later I developed a terror of the devil and Satanists (good old catholic church). The bigger the world became the more things I discovered that were to cause me anxiety and panic. I don't fly, I don't go in lifts, I hate heights, I get claustrophobic, it just went (goes) on and on and on. Fear keeps you trapped and imprisoned, welcome to my cage.

The planet dies or we blow it up

By the time we formed Zounds in the second half of the 1970s there was a lot to be frightened of. I learned how the State kept people in check through a combination of tacit consent and fear, mostly fear. Fear of war, fear of terrorism, fear of the lights going out, fear of 'the other'. By this point I had been busted twice for dope, and every time I went out at night I was stopped by the Police. It really was tiring, and my resentment towards the police, their thuggish behaviour and their constant harassment of our little crew, grew in proportion to my fear of them. The cells really freaked me out. I just don't like being locked in a stone room with a twelve-inch thick door and no access to the outside world. Anything could happen in there. Others had it worse I guess. Certainly the black, inner city kids had to put up with a lot of shit. They were disproportionately targeted by 'police gangs' such as the S.P.G. in London, and The West Midlands Serious Crime Squad in and around Birmingham. These units, which were eventually disbanded, were notoriously brutal. They got away with their discriminatory behaviour using the cover of the discredited 'sus laws'. Also now defunct.

It all came as a bit of a shock to me. I couldn't see what harm we were doing, and could never understand why we were such a focus of police attention. All we did was smoke dope, play music and talk bollocks. I suppose big, strong policemen trained in unarmed combat found it easier to hassle stoned, innocent kids than they did to go up against genuine villains. The more we saw and experienced this kind of thing, the more oppositional we became. I started to notice all the other areas of society where official institutions acted unfairly, and often cruelly. You started paying more attention to stories of corruption, nepotism and privilege. How it was all kept in place by the ultimate threat, violence.

Outside the microcosm of our day-to-day lives, the cold war was dragging on and on. The West and the Soviet Bloc were engaged in a nuclear weapons programme based on 'Mutually Assured Destruction' (M.A.D.). Both sides were fed endless propaganda about how the other side wanted to destroy them and their way of life. Fear of an outside enemy makes government restrictions and control even easier. If a government plays its cards right it can even get the people to demand increased surveillance, tighter controls and infringements of liberty. It's all there in Orwell's 1984. It wasn't for nothing people were starting to refer to the U.K. as Airstrip One. Especially when it was announced that U.S. Cruise missiles were going to be stationed at an airbase near you.

Despite a number of badly covered up nuclear accidents, the government pressed ahead with its civil nuclear power programme. None of us were persuaded that this was in any way safe or viable. Even if it was, the government and its agencies had such a long record of lies and misinformation regarding nuclear energy, that one's natural inclination was to be very wary of the veracity of government safety claims. When in 1979 a partial meltdown of the core at Three Mile Island in Harrisburg, USA happened our concerns seemed validated.

Global corporations were consolidating. More and more stuff was under the control of fewer and fewer huge companies. These conglomerates had no allegiance to any country, any people, or the ecological and social environment. Nothing but the bottom line seemed to concern them. Slowly the corporations were starting to transform everywhere into everywhere else. Eventually all towns would become the same with their Ikeas, McDonalds, Niketowns, Starbucks and Disney Stores.

All of these situations were further compounded by a social and physical landscape that was being further scarred by an economic decline and various other symptoms of the 'end of empire'. The most repellant of these being the rise of the National Front with their racist agenda and fascist sympathies. Fuelled by the racist statements of Enoch Powell, Margaret Thatcher and other top

Conservative politicians of the day, quasi-fascist parties such as the National Front, were organising street demos and violent affray. This was further stoked up by a repetition of racist imagery in newspapers such as the Sun and the Daily Mail who were running campaigns around 'mugging and street robbery'.

Let's face it, for someone of a nervous disposition, and a tendency towards a dramatic interpretation of events, there was a fuck of a lot to be frightened of in the late 1970s. I admire those people who say 'I would rather die on my feet than live on my knees'. I wish I could be more like them, but sadly I am one of those who would rather live on my knees sucking cock than die. Because death is the great fear that tops all others.

07 DID HE JUMP OR WAS HE PUSHED

Who was that on the window ledge?
Did he jump or was he pushed?
He left a note which no one read
In desperate hand the note just said:
"Never turned my back on society
Society turned its back on me.
Never tried once to drop out,
I just couldn't get in from the start."

The children all played clever games
The grown-ups gave them clever names
Turned them all from very young
On to the drug competition
Feed them TV everyday
Teach them just how they should play
For the ones that start to stray
Cut them off till they obey

Our little friend was not the type
To want to have to stand and fight
Bully boys all could pick
Upon the lonely little kid
The grown ups all looked hard and long
Said "He's got two feet he can stand on
We never liked the sickly ones
The boisterous ones are much more fun"

He found it hard to socialise
Cos when he laughed or when he cried
In the wrong place he'd be chastised
An idiot to be despised
Never learnt to play the game
The way that you're supposed to play
Never learnt the things to say
Or lock emotion safe away

Who was that on the window ledge?
Did he jump or was he pushed?
He left a note which no one read
In desperate hand the note just said:

"Never turned my back on society
Society turned its back on me.
All the world cannot be wrong
It must be me I don't belong."
"All the world cannot be wrong
It must be me I don't belong"
"All the world cannot be wrong
It must be me I don't belong"
"All the world cannot be wrong

08 THE UNFREE CHILD

The unfree child is full of woe
Into the unfree adult he will grow
Have unfree children of its own
On and on and so it goes

Take your hands from off your genitals
Eat those greens and grow up strong
Don't piss yourself it's very naughty
Stephen, Stephen don't you shine
Don't speak now we are talking
Not a word less you disgrace
There's people listening
Don't embarrass us
And never let us catch you masturbate

09 MY MUMMYS GONE

When I was a baby my mummy told me
If I was a bad boy daddy would scold me
When I was a baby my mummy lectured
If I was a good boy I would be rewarded

Mummy, daddy, am I what you expected
In your eyes am I to be respected
Did you want me or just want a reflection
Of the values that you hold and the way you see them
My mummy's gone
To a place where I can't go
A place that's cloaked in the mystery
Of corporate identity
Supermarkets and three piece suits
My mummy's gone
My mummy's gone

When I was a little girl my mummy told me
Had to make an effort to make myself pretty
Got to get a husband, got to have a baby
Got to be a credit to the rest of the family

Now that I'm older, I know that you scarred me
But I don't hold it against you, though it damage
me sorely
I know you're a victim just, just like me
You can feel the pressure just, just like me

Did He Jump Or Was He Pushed - The Unfree Child - My Mummy's Gone

Described by some kindly soul on youtube as: -

'A long, sprawling eight minute epic which puts forward intellectual anarchist ideas of childhood and the conformity implicit in the systems educational structures. The best thing about this song is the accessible way in which they manage to put forward such complex ideas, and also the beautifully discordant guitars that run alongside the lyrics, reaching a crescendo towards the end. I never thought much of The Zounds' other work but this song is a sure fire hit for me and resonates both intellectually and musically with me in a big way. Simply brilliant.'

Nice of him to say so. But these three songs were never intended as either a political statement or an analysis of the relationship between the State and the child. It was simply a collection of pieces that described experiences I'd witnessed endlessly in the playgrounds, streets, schools and homes where I grew up. Of course, it is political, because all songs are political, even the ones that just go on endlessly about how they are going to love their baby 'awll night lawng....'

Whilst I would never claim anything for my own songs, I think the appeal of this is the same as many other songs that deal with depressing subject matter. As the subject here is teenage suicide, it couldn't be much more depressing. I find songs concerning tragedy and loss can actually be uplifting and life-affirming. Sometimes it is helpful to know that other people feel the hurt and the pain too. Though I have often felt alienated and disconnected from the world, songs that express those sentiments help to remind me that I am not alone or unique in finding it hard to cope with the insensitivity and harshness of things. Music seems to do that more than any art form for me, for most people I think.

Over the years childhood has come up in my songs a number of times. It took me years to get over the trauma of childhood, or rather, to see it in some kind of perspective. My experiences then, still influence the way I react to situations today. No doubt Dr Freud and his disciples would have many a well-paid field day working out why and how, if I was so fucking clever and all knowing on the subject, I made such a mess of bringing up my own kids.

This little suite of songs is often one of the highlights of our live shows, which is eternally gratifying as a lot of the audience at Zounds gigs tend to like to jump around to the fast ones, and this veers dangerously close to the horrors of prog with it's dreamy intro, different vocal leads and severe tempo and mood changes.

The female voice on the record is that of Gina from The Raincoats. The producer got her in as a way of making £30 for one of his mates. Fair enough, I like to think I would do the same. Sadly though, I always thought her voice was too posh, and I found the way she pronounced the word 'masturbate' laughable.

10 LITTLE BIT MORE

Rain is flooding, the pavement cracks
Headlines screaming 'Pay more tax'
A girl is crying as she misses her train
Weather man is saying "Just a little more rain"

Little bit more - Little bit more
Everybody's looking for a little bit more

Glass is blowing, the wind don't care
It will blow on anything you leave down there
I just don't believe the price of things
Weather man is saying "Just a little more wind"

Little bit more - Little bit more
Everybody's looking for a little bit more

Time runs quick like an engine train
Someone's asking to increase some claim
If I had more hours I think I'd feel fine
Weather man's saying "Just a little more time"
Little bit more - Little bit more
Everybody's looking for a little bit more

Little Bit More

People say you should listen to your body more,
but my body is often telling me to have a joint, a cup of
coffee and a bar of chocolate, then go and lay down and
listen to some Billy Childish records.

It's a bit of an odd one this, lyrically more oblique than many of the songs. I think I must have had Bob Dylan in my head a lot at the time I wrote it. It was probably a conscious decision to use the word 'weatherman' in the song, to deliberately reference his great anarchist declamation 'Subterranean Homesick Blues'. The fact that he was supposedly referencing the U.S. revolutionary sect of the same name made it richer for me. I like doing that, using words that have a number of significations. As a writer I think it's something you do for yourself; not many people are going to get most of these obscure cultural links. It's a bit of a conceit I suppose, trying to associate yourself with great and interesting things, so that some of the reflected glory might stick. Other times though, you just use any old word that rhymes.

I think at the time I was struck by the fact that I, like most people, always seemed to need a little bit more than they had. Everything was geared up to wanting more anyway. Desire was nurtured in the magazines, newspapers and TV channels. Not just in the commercials, but in the lifestyle sections, the travel sections, the pullout supplements, in fiction and nonfiction alike.

It's not that everyone is greedy. It's just that no one ever seemed to have quite all they needed or desired. All they required to make their life complete was a little bit more. Though when, and if, you got it, somehow it was still not quite enough, and actually you still needed, just a little bit more.

Maybe that's what is meant by economic growth. Everyone put into a state of perpetual desire for material fulfilment, so the amount of stuff in the world keeps growing. I never really grasped politics or economics at a technical level, and from what we have found out since, it has become obvious that no other fucker has either. Whether they be financier, banker, economist, professor or investigative journalist, it is a complete mystery to them all.

11 THIS LAND

This land is your land and this land is my land
From the dirty water of the river Thames
To the rusting cranes of the Tees and the Tyne
The land that's choking with wires and plugs
Strangled with fences and stuck with knives
Was this land made for you and me?

This town is your town and this town is my town
From the derelict slums that are dirty and grey
To the house on the hill in the private estate
The places nice kids would never go
To the places no-one else has the right to go
Was this land made for you and me?
Made for you and me

This street is your street and this street is my street
From the broken phone box where the gangs all meet
To the glass on the path that cuts your feet
From the neighbours next door who refuse to speak
To the cop in the Hunter doing his beat
Was this land made for you and me?

It's your world too you can do what you want
It's your world too, it's your world too...

This Land

Woody Guthrie / John Steinbeck / The Grapes Of Wrath

I feel linked to people and things that happened before my time, things in history. Not through race, nationality, religion; those are fictional and divisive categories. More through ideas and through artistic expression. I always wanted to know what went before.

I was about 14 when I came across Woody Guthrie, maybe younger. Because we always had country music in our house, we were aware of a lot of American folk stuff. Also, when at a tender age, you start hearing stuff on the radio by Bob Dylan, The Byrds, The Lovin' Spoonful, Simon and Garfunkel and other folk rock and protest stuff, eventually you are going to be led back to Woody Guthrie. One of the great writer/performers and champions of the common people. I guess I really got into him from about the age of sixteen or seventeen though. After I read John Steinbeck's emotionally shattering novel 'The Grapes Of Wrath'. The novel traces the journey of dispossessed farm workers from the ecological disaster of the Oklahoma dust bowl, to the poisoned-paradise of Californian labour camps, company stores, private police forces and strikebreakers. The book blew my head off, it opened up history and beautifully described the power relations and brutality of Capitalism at its most raw. And it was intimately connected with Woody Guthrie's dust bowl songs. It made me see Guthrie's songs in a bigger context. It brought them more alive and brought him more alive. It brought the world more alive, and it powerfully demonstrated the way songs and art are intimately connected with the social and political world. Both Steinbeck's novel, and Guthrie's songs, connected 'man-made' environmental pillage with the exploitation of working people, and the excesses and perpetuation of privilege amongst the capital owning classes. They threw light on the way workers are set against each other in competition for barely adequate jobs and housing, how the desperation can lead to self hatred, violence, alcoholism and drug dependency. But they were not depressing or negative because they also carried a message of hope and resistance, a message that emphasised the strength and warmth of solidarity and co-operation. The songs showed us that the pleasures and expressions of ordinary people were as rich and potent and significant as those of any highbrow culture belonging to the bosses and masters.

Woody Guthrie wrote the song 'This Land Is Your Land' and within it described the paradise that the USA could be. But the song also tells us that while the land is in the shadow of 'the City' (financial institutions), with its accent on 'private property', then it is paradise lost.

I wrote the Zounds song 'This Land' because there are many themes and ideas in Woody's songs that bear revisiting, repeating, developing, and paying tribute to. The hope is of course that one day they will be irrelevant and we won't need to sing them. A day that is either a long way off or never going to come.

12 NEW BAND

There's a new band every week
New ways to move your feet
New sounds to thrill your ears
Same old chords dressed up weird
New attitudes, brand new stance
Different steps but the same old dance
New ways but in the end
It's a new way to make you spend

The media cares cause the media knows
Fashions comes and fashions go
Last week's trend is now passé
Cause there's something better to buy today
You can buy something and leave it at that
But you go and try to take it back
They'll offer you nothing though it cost the Earth
Soon show you what they think you're worth

And there's a new band every week
New ways to move your feet
New ways but in the end
It's a new way to make you spend

Been searching for some thing but I don't know what, been
searching for a long, long time
Then someone comes along and says "this is it", but it
will cost you realise
You pay your money, try your luck, think your trust them
one more time
But how long does it take to feel you're being ripped
off, there's always something new to buy

There's a new band every week
New ways to move your feet
New ways but in the end
It's a new way to make you spend
New band, it's a new band
New band, new band

New Band

Punk/Rock is dead - the thrill of the new, the shock of the old - consume me baby - you are what you eat

Some women have suggested to me, that the way some men relate to the minutiae of rock n roll, i.e. fascination with line-ups, labels, release dates and associated paraphernalia, shows them to be emotionally retarded, perpetual adolescents. The argument usually develops along the lines that these men are probably using rock n roll to fill a cold, gaping void in their meaningless and unfulfilled, personal lives. They might even go on to claim that it is in the same order as train spotting, stamp collecting and making models of the Empire State Building out of match sticks. It is possible they are right and I plead guilty as charged. My endless, tedious obsession with rock music and the people who play it meant that during the 1970s and early 1980s I would read all the music press all the time. Like everyone with the infatuation, I was most besotted with the NME. It didn't invent punk rock, but it gave it impetus, to the point where it was name checked in the Sex Pistols first single 'Anarchy In The UK'.

The 'year zero' of punk rock was a seminal time of new beginnings. New possibilities, new growth, everything was remade and remodelled. And it was all charted and detailed by the clever dicks at the NME. Ushered in by the likes of Nick Kent, Mick Farren, Charles Shaar Murray and Max Bell, and then ratcheted up by young guns such as Paul Morley, Parsons and Burchill, Ian Penman, and briefly, our own beloved Jonathan Barnett

Of course, we now know that punk was not a brave new dawn, but the sound of the last rites being administered, over the last throw of the dying rock-corpse. It was the end of rock music and the conclusion of an era that started in the 1950s. There might have been a few good bands since, but basically, as a vibrant, original, ground breaking, semi-cohesive, musical and social force it was dead in the water. As dead as Swing Jazz and Skiffle.

Frankly I think no-one under the age of 50 should be allowed to play rock music. They should certainly not be allowed to own guitars. That is an ancient art and should be left to the ancients to practice it. If you were not already doing it by 1980 then that's it. Younger people have their synthesisers and drum machines, computers and I-things, samplers, modules, nodules, podules and digitoys. You must be able to do wonderful things with those. But kids, rock n roll is for the ghosts.

Punk gave way to 'new wave', 'no-wave', 'post-punk' and 'alternative'. It eventually culminated in the insipid graveyard of white-boy-rock that is laughingly referred to as 'indie'. Strange to think that 'indie' used to signify an economic relationship. It described a situation where bands were releasing records independently of major music producers and distributors. Eventually it just came to mean boys in skinny jeans, whose mums bought them guitars and drove them to gigs and practices.

The NME, and the other music papers, would carry endless articles about yet another new sensation, new Beatles, new Dylan, new Pistols, new Clash, new Bowie. Every week some weird and wonderful genre, or movement, or haircut alliance, would be thrust into the limelight. This week 'New Romantics', next week Salsa, Latin and the Modern Beatniks, look out, here comes 'Blue-Eyed Soul', closely followed by 'Industrial Funk' and New Goth. Suddenly all the stuff you were into last week is redundant and worthless. A constant flow of new trends work their way into the market. Trends that are either spotted on the street, incorporated into the cultural industries, then sold back to 'the street', or are manufactured by cynical 'creatives', then foisted on the public through high profile advertising and product placement. But it is not just in music. It is in everything, clothes, garden furniture, razors, washing powder, electronic goods, baby food. It never ends.

Sell! Sell! Sell! That is ultimately what it's about. And in the West, even the poorest households are now rammed with clutter and stuff. Old stuff, broken stuff, new stuff, stuff for the weekends, stuff for this, stuff for that, and everyone's got fucking stuff coming out of their bloody ears.

Yet no matter how up to date you get, before you know it something new has been introduced onto the scene and you're behind the times again. Radio, phonograph, cinema, television, stereo, colour, cassette player, 8-track cartridge, VHS, Betamax,

Laserdisc, CD, DVD, Blue Ray, IPod, HD, 3D, wi-fi, PC, surround-sound, hologram. It will never end.

There should certainly be a moratorium on inventions. No-one can cope with the stuff we've got now, so we certainly don't need any more.

13 DIRTY SQUATTERS

Some dirty squatters moved into my street
With their non sexist haircuts and their dirty feet
Their dogs, cats, political elite
They may have beds but they don't use sheets
Furnishing their houses from the contents of skips
Things that decent people put on rubbish tips
They look quite harmless sitting out in the sun
But I wouldn't let my daughter marry one

Dirty squatters
Oh my god they're moving in next door
Dirty squatters
Is it for people like this that Winston won - the war

I've lived in this street for nearly fifteen years
Lived here with my hopes, lived here with my fears
Paid my taxes, paid my bills
Watched my money vanish in the council tills
Along come these scruffs with their education
Their grand ideas, talk of corruption
My rent keeps rising, my job gets boring
If things gets worse then I'm gonna have to join them

Dirty squatters
Oh my god they're moving in next door
Dirty squatters
Is it for people like this that Winston won - the war

Bought myself a lock and late tonight
Under the cover of darkness if the moons not bright
Getting out of here, moving next door
Don't think I can take much more

Dirty squatters
Oh my god they're moving in next door
Dirty squatters
Is it for people like this that Winston won …

Dirty Squatters

Lou Reed wrote songs about heroin and transvestism -
Iggy Pop wrote songs about sadomasochism -
I wrote songs about social housing

In the 1970s and 1980s squatting was a necessity. There were thousands of squatters in England at that time, many of them in London. It wasn't a choice, there was no choice. Where else could we live? We had no money for private rented accommodation, and there was no council provision for single people. Local councils didn't like squatters and would sometimes smash up their own houses to make them uninhabitable. They would pour concrete down the toilets and remove electricity connections and wiring. You would often see signs painted across empty houses that read, 'LEB OFF'. This would be done by squatter activists who were letting other potential squatters know that the London Electricity Board connections had been dismantled. It was local government that vandalised property; most squatters would actually repair and renovate the houses.

I squatted in a number of places, mainly in Islington and Hackney, but there were squatter communities all over the capital. We had a cool squat in Grimaldi House, on the Priory Green Estate in Kings Cross, for a while. It was grimy and seedy but we liked it a lot. Then I moved up to a place off the New North Road, which is where I wrote Dirty Squatters.

There were so many empty houses about then. I was going out with a Spanish woman called Conchita. She lived in Hackney, off Broadway Market. The street was called Brougham Road. There were a load of anarchists and activists and communists, and some 'separatist' women's houses there. There were a lot of 'ists' around at that time. In those days Broadway Market was rough, depressed and grim. There was some famous graffiti there which read, 'Broadway Market is not a sinking ship it is a submarine'. Now Broadway Market is trendy and yuppified.

Dave Morris, who later found celebrity when McDonalds

unsuccessfully sued him, lived there. He was going off to ferment revolution some place overseas, and said I could move into the squat he was vacating. Joseph moved in next door and we built a practice room there and it became Zounds headquarters. There was a disused bus garage around the corner that got squatted by a load of travellers with their buses and vans, which seemed poetically just. A stone's throw across London Fields there were other houses occupied by Genesis P. Orridge from Throbbing Gristle/Psychic TV, and people from avant-rock band 23 Skidoo. It was a very creative environment.

Mostly I remember the summers. It was hot. Our houses faced south, towards the towers of the City of London financial district. The other side of the street had been demolished. A corrugated iron fence had been erected and behind it was a construction site where a new housing development was being built. The corrugated iron was graffitied with A's in circles, CND signs, and all manner of arcane symbols and messages. There was dust everywhere and in everything, on really hot days it was like the desert. In many people's eyes Brougham Road was to anarcho-punk what Haight Ashbury was to hippies, or Greenwich Village was to the protest music scene.

Joseph refutes it was a scene at all, but then he is very matter of fact and down to earth. I, on the other hand, prefer to see the drama and the long sweep of history in what is occurring at any given time. To me it was a place where some like-minded individuals and groups came together and engaged in common activity. At that time there was no such term as 'anarcho-punk'. That was coined after Zounds disbanded for the first time. I saw it as latter day incarnation in a long line of English and international radicals and bohemians, stretching back at least to Gerard Winstanley and the Diggers. I thought we were carrying on a radical, utopian tradition, and was proud to be doing so. Maybe this all sounds a bit grandiose today, but at that period I really did believe we were building an alternative society. Joseph has been quoted as declaring it was just a few hungry children huddling together to keep warm. I suppose it shows that Joseph had a bit more of a grip on reality than I did.

Good squatters / bad squatters

Of course, not all squatters are the high-minded, socially responsible, idealised type, I like to promote. My first experience of squatting was in Reading in 1974. It was a classic Daily Mail style, suburban, nightmare situation. Some people I knew found an empty house on Kendrick Avenue. I had a bedsit nearby. They moved in en masse and started having parties straight away. The problem was, the house wasn't actually empty, it was partially furnished and the owner was away on a recuperating holiday after a traumatic separation from his wife. He was devastated when he returned to be denied entry and have to witness his lovely house wrecked. The place soon became a magnet for all of Reading's detritus. There were a lot of strong drugs and a lot of weak people hanging out there. It started off really nicely, with us taking acid and climbing out onto a scaffolding platform that for some reason had been erected outside the attic window. Astounding, now I wouldn't go out on anything that high up, certainly not while tripping, and I certainly couldn't take acid now. I can hardly cope with being in the same room as someone who is tripping.

Very quickly though, the happy, acid daze gave way to the chill and bitter storm of methamphetamine, and to all the haphazard and uncontrollable madness that is its handmaiden. At the time there was a glut of very pure and powerful speed circulating in Reading, the rumour was that it was stolen and imported from Spain, and it was in limited supply.

A couple of the people hanging round the squat had come into some money on their eighteenth birthdays. I think it was compensation for childhood accidents. I don't know how much it was, a few hundred quid probably. It all went on methamphetamine, purchased from The Star pub in Reading. The Star was where we all got our start in the drug scene. It was heavy, and the main dealers were a Nigerian called Skinny and a Jamaican called Shine. Nice guys, but volatile. They inhabited a world that was mysterious, dangerous and ultimately unattractive to us little white lambs. Skinny and Shine gave a lot of us adventurous white kids our introduction to the world of drugs. Not that they were encouraging us, we didn't need any encouragement. They were just the ones with the goodies.

We flashed and careered our way through the next month in a methamphetamine frenzy. The squat, which had started off clean and ordered and bright, became dark, dilapidated and disgusting. The police raided it one night, prompting someone to hurriedly stash a lump of hash down the overflow of the bathroom sink. Once the cops had gone he had to dismantle the sink and the pipe work to retrieve the contraband. He managed to completely wreck the plumbing and create a dank, horrible, smelly no go area, where the bathroom and toilet used to be. There was no more water in the place after that. Things got very dirty.

One night someone found a load of pornographic magazines in a cupboard. Some of the guys (this was mainly a male scene) started to attack the 'girly pictures' with carving knives. All the while screaming abuse at the naked images. It became quite frenzied and misogynistic. Disturbing. Then we found some glue and a hammer and nails. A couple of people got it into their heads to glue the pots and pans to the kitchen surfaces. Then they nailed the drawers and the cupboard doors shut. Why this seemed so hilarious I can't remember.

A youth called Snake moved onto the scene and into the squat. He was a skinhead who had just got out of juvenile prison. These days he would probably be classified as someone with learning difficulties or special needs. One night he took a few of the lads down to the kitchens of St Joseph's Convent Girls' School. The idea was to steal food and bring it back to the squat. They broke in, Snake promptly shat on the floor, then they shipped back loads of provisions to the squat. God knows why, we never ate anything except for speed and acid.

One night a couple of us went for a walk with Snake. We came across an open-top Jaguar sports car. There was a briefcase in the back seat and keys in the ignition. Some people are very trusting, some people are very dumb. Snake couldn't resist. He invited us to join him in a joy ride. We politely declined. We may have been out of our minds on speed, but we weren't stupid. Snake roared off. He turned up at the squat 2 days later in a new pair of colourfully patched, leather trousers, very fashionable in the early 1970s. Apparently he had written off the Jag near Basingstoke. Being unharmed, he stole money and a credit card from a briefcase left in the car, then hitched to London. He bought the trousers in the King's Road then hitched back to Reading, turning up with a load of bottles of wine, more booty from the stolen credit card. How anyone would have thought that a juvenile delinquent like Snake could legitimately have a credit card in those days beggars belief.

But they were innocent times and we had to make our own fun.

Eventually the compensation money ran out and the Spanish methamphetamine dried up. We then started combing the Chemist shops of Reading, buying up Benzedrine inhalers. These could be broken open to reveal a big wodge of cotton wool. The cotton wool was soaked in Benzedrine. You just ate the cotton wool and you got an incredibly powerful hit. Much stronger than the cheap sulphate that usually did the rounds in places like Reading. At this point it was rumoured that one of our gang knew a girl in Southampton. With the last of our friend's money we hired a Ford Transit for the weekend and about a dozen of us set off for Southampton in a very cramped van. When we got there it became apparent that the fantasist who claimed to know a girl didn't actually know where she lived. Exhausted and withdrawing from the speed frenzy we all crammed into the back of the Transit and tried to sleep.

At some point during that night I was aware that someone was shaking me awake. I also became aware that I was screaming uncontrollably. I tried to gather myself, apologised and closed my eyes. Then I couldn't work out if I'd just imagined it or whether it had really happened. 'Did you just wake me up and was I screaming' I enquired of no-one in particular. The reply was affirmative. I closed my eyes again, and then I had a slightly clichéd vision. In my mind I could see myself knocking on the open door of a doctor's surgery. I saw the doctor turn to me and say, 'Ah, you can come in now Stephen, you are mad'. Clichéd or not, it scared me shitless. As I finally fell into unconscious slumber I resolved to quit this crazy scene as soon as I got back to Reading.

I still had the bed-sit, so when I got back I went in and didn't answer the door to anyone for three weeks. Debby Webb would come round and feed me, while the rest of the time I sat in silence, chain smoking roll-ups and listening to the radio. I discovered Radio 4. I had never heard it before, but it was so cosy and warm and middle class, it proved to be the ideal antidote to rampant speed-freak insanity, and violent skinheads with special needs. The best thing about that little period was that a guy called Andy borrowed some money off me, he couldn't pay it back, so he gave me the first Velvet Underground album instead. Appropriate I think.

The music

When I came up with the chords and tune for Dirty Squatters, I think I was trying to get that jarring, discordant weirdness that was a feature of some of Captain Beefheart's music. Obviously the Captain was in a different league to me, and to take Leonard Cohen's metaphor, I was a thousand floors beneath him in the 'tower of song'. But it was an influence.

14 LOADS OF NOISE

Well the news is on, I listen all day
It's stranger than fiction that they make up these days
The music is crap, that the radio plays
I know it for certain, it's true like all clichés

The kids are making loads of noise outside on the street
tonight
They're stealing cars, crashing them, Cortinas, Jags and
anything - that moves

The phone-ins are stupid and sometimes they're sad
All the people that call in they are totally mad
The interviewer so certain, so smug and so right
Cut you off in a second, shut you down when he like

The kids are making loads of noise outside on the street
tonight
They're stealing cars, crashing them, Cortinas, Jags and
anything

All the D.J.'s play records, keep a permanent smile
Can they be that happy, so much of the while
Do they think we're so stupid, so useless and dumb
That we need their inanities to have a little fun

The kids are making loads of noise outside on the street
tonight
They're stealing cars, crashing them, Cortinas, Jags and
anything - that moves, that moves

Loads Of Noise

24 Hour psychedelic art party – The dole – Joy riding –
Council estates & car factories – Theology students

Zounds grew out of a group of people from around East Berkshire. In about 1976 we moved up to Oxford. When we arrived we started to lose ourselves in a fuzzy world of marijuana, political conspiracy theories and total-24hour-non-stop-party-art-experience. Although we had no money we got by OK. Tripping and skipping through the meadows and waterways and the old medieval buildings. It was all psychedelically gentle and Lewis Carroll-esque. There were a lot of people around with money, drugs, enthusiasm and ideas, so it didn't matter that much if, like us, you were poor and living on the dole. We bedded in with the local bohemians and the Polytechnic and (to a lesser extent) University students. If you had a few wits about you and something interesting to contribute, you could fit in and be taken along for the ride.

Living on the dole was a lifestyle choice in that era. I have already explained that working was not a viable option for tender flowers such as we were. It didn't fit in with our sleep and play routine. Looking back I liken the dole to an institution such as the Arts Council, only for rock bands and freaks. If you had a middle class sensibility, a grasp on funding mechanisms, an art school background, and the wherewithal to find and fill in application forms, it was possible to extract funding for art and music from the State. But we were so detached we wouldn't have even known those things existed. And even if we did we certainly couldn't have conceived they would be open to us. The dole allowed you to sleep a large part of the day and then get up and play music, paint, sculpt and engage in productive play. We thought everybody should go on it.

But there was another side to Oxford that rarely impinged upon our rejectionist lives. On the outskirts of the 'dreaming spires' is a place called Cowley. It was one of the homes of the car building industry in England, and British Leyland housed one of its main factories there. Cowley is also the location of the Blackbird Leys Estate. This is one of the largest council estates in Europe. We didn't go there much. Oxford is up the Thames from where I was brought up in Reading. The council estate, factory-work culture of Cowley was something I was trying to escape from. Not many of the people I was mixing with in Oxford were from my background, so for me Blackbird Leys, and its factory world, were a bit too close for comfort. I didn't want to be too close to its orbit, in case it sucked me in and kept me captive.

Blackbird Leys is most famous for its contribution to the pastime that became known as 'joy-riding'. Stealing cars, doing stunts in them, racing them and finally, crashing them. All for a delighted audience of spectators from the local area. Many places engage in these activities, but Blackbird Leys lays claim to being the place where it all started in a big way.

One time I did go there was to play a gig with a strange, vaguely aristocratic ex-theology student I had come into contact with. He told me he had been studying to become a priest but had given it all up to become a pub entertainer. We turned up at a dilapidated 1960s style pub. It looked more like a health centre waiting room than it did an Inn on the outskirts of Oxford. The place was rammed with working class families. A lot of drink was being taken and I really didn't feel the part. In fact, I expected to get a good kicking before the night was out. We set up and did some rock n roll songs, a few folk numbers and some Leadbelly and Woody Guthrie tunes. We also managed a few waltzes and Music Hall numbers. I was astounded to realise it was going down a storm. People even sang along if they knew the stuff. I was convinced none of this was my doing, it was just that there was something in the manner of this seemingly ineffectual, ex-theologist that gently connected with people in the pub.

I'm not one for pushing my luck though, so I never played there with him again. I did use the imagery of the area for the chorus of Loads Of Noise, which was essentially a song about the radio.

15 TARGET

I was living rather quietly by my village in the trees
Don't bother anybody and they don't bother me
I'm always kind to passers-by,
I never make a fuss
Considerate of my neighbours so they don't bother us

I don't mean to be unsociable but time's my only wealth
So I continue to live quietly, keep myself unto myself

One day while feeling lonely I wandered into town
To take a look and listen to what was going down
Nothing seemed to change much, all looked just the same
So I went about my business till the sky began to rain

I took shelter in a doorway and started to peruse
Through a local paper to check up on the news
Hit me like a hammer, the headline jumped and screeched
My home was now a target for a missile from the east

The Americans are coming, they're bringing us their bombs
To aim them at their enemies from our little island home
I don't want to die because of some mad president's whim
I don't want to be a part of a war no one can win

You're welcome here Americans
We love you but not your bombs
Welcome here Americans
We love you but not your bombs...

Welcome here Americans
We love you but not your bombs
And not your lies
You're welcome here!

16 MR DISNEY

Oh! Mr. Disney where are you now?
Will good overcome evil the way that you tell?
Oh! Mr. Disney where have you gone?
Mickey's being threatened by a neutron bomb
Oh! Mr. Disney what you gonna do?
Your film's no longer seem quite so red, white and blue
Oh! Mr. Disney how does it seem?
Now your films are being shown in radiation green

Target - Mr Disney

I swapped my mum for a cruise missile - Women

I wrote this on the beach in Kent just up the coast from Dungeness Nuclear Power Station. Everything was Cold-War and CND in those days. Cruise missiles were on the horizon and getting closer everyday. This would provoke women activists and peaceniks to form protest camps outside the US Airbase at Greenham Common and similar locations.

These would occasionally be the focus of huge demonstrations by women who would circle the base, holding hands and chanting. Echoing events like those of 21st October 1967 in Washington, when hippies tried to levitate the Pentagon, and held up mirrors to reflect the evil back at itself.

Strangely, my mother used to teach ballroom dancing to US soldiers at Greenham Common and other U.S.A.F. bases in the early 1960s. She ended up marrying one and going to live in the USA. I lost a mother but gained a Cruise missile with a devastating Nuclear Warhead. Probably a fare swap knowing my mother.

Mr Disney? At the time I thought Hollywood was just the propaganda arm of the US Military Industrial Complex. I think I might have been right.

Timeline from BBC news website

The Greenham Common Women's Peace Camp carried out huge numbers of demonstrations. Hundreds of arrests were made and the resultant court action was often complicated and controversial. BBC News Online looks at some of the key points from the camp's 19-year history.

September 1981:
The Women for Life on Earth march reaches Greenham Common to protest about NATO's decision to site cruise missiles at Greenham Common.

March 1982:
The first blockade of the base is staged by 250 women and 34 arrests are made.

May 1982:
The first eviction of the peace camp takes place and four arrests are made as bailiffs and police move in an attempt to clear the women and their possessions from the site. The camp relocates.

December 1982: 30,000 women join hands to 'embrace the base'.

January 1983:
Newbury District Council revokes the common land byelaws for Greenham Common. It makes itself private landlord for the site and starts court proceedings to reclaim eviction costs from women whose address is given on the electoral role as the peace camp. Byelaws restricting access to the camp were ruled illegal by the house of lords in 1990.

November 1983:
The first of the cruise missiles arrives at Greenham Common airbase. A total of 95 missiles are to follow in the coming months.

April 1983:
70,000 CND supporters form a 14-mile human chain linking Burghfield, Aldermaston and Greenham. 200 women dressed as furry animals enter the base to stage a protest picnic.

December 1983:
50,000 women encircle the base, holding up mirrors. Parts of the fence are brought down and hundreds of arrests are made.

1987:
Presidents Ronald Reagan and Mikhail Gorbachev sign the Intermediate-range Nuclear Forces (INF) Treaty - the first agreement between the two powers to actually reduce weaponry. It spelt the end for the Cruise missile and similar Soviet weapons in eastern Europe.

Supporters of the Reagan administration, dismissing the role of the peace campaigners, hailed the Treaty as a victory for the president's "zero option" of 1981.

At that time, President Reagan sanctioned building up nuclear forces in western Europe until both sides would agree to remove all of their respective intermediate weapons.

August 1989:
The first cruise missile leaves Greenham Common.

March 1991:
The US completes removal of all Greenham Common Cruise missiles and the Soviet Union makes reciprocal reductions to its stockpiles in Warsaw Pact countries under the INF treaty.

In total, 2,692 weapons are eliminated - 846 US missiles based across Western Europe and 1,846 Soviet missiles across Eastern Europe.

30 September 1992:
The American airforce leaves Greenham Common.

1 January 2000:
Peace campaigners plan to welcome in the new millennium in Greenham, and then the women still living at Greenham plan to leave.

17 DANCING

It's nineteen thirty-three
And she don't wanna know
About little men and things
Cause she just wanna go
Dancing, dancing

She walks the street by day
Less people all around
But she don't worry about that
Cause she is going downtown

She's going dancing, dancing
Making a noise
Dancing, dancing
Girls and the boys
Dancing, dancing
Dancing, dancing

Munich, Berlin Cologne
Sweet mother Germany
Come to the cabaret
Don't worry about history

Dancing, dancing
Girls and the boys
Dancing, dancing
Making a noise

It's nineteen thirty-eight
Sweet mother Germany
It seems so far away
And she will never be
Dancing, dancing
The girls and the boys
Dancing, dancing
Making a noise
Dancing, dancing,
Never again,
Never never never again
Never

Dancing

War – Books – Germany, ancient and modern –
Krautrock – Berlin wall and the cold war –
The Clash meet Zounds, nothing happens

This song takes place in inter-war Germany. It is an anti-fascist song. Germany plays a massive role in the deep, psychohistory of the English (British?). Maybe it's the same in other places, I don't know.

When growing up in England in the 1960s you were dwarfed by the massive, undiminishing shadow of World War Two. It was a constant part of the cultural landscape; films, comedy shows, jokes, Remembrance Sundays, the reminiscences of parents and grandparents, on and on it went.

We didn't have many books in our house, maybe a dozen, certainly no more than 15. One we did have was 'The Scourge Of The Swastika' by Lord Russell of Liverpool. I never read it, but I would sometimes take it out and look at the photographs in the middle. They were of the Auschwitz death camp at the moment of liberation. Wretched, broken people, all skin and bones with empty eyes, hollow cheeks and heads too big for their bodies. There they were, staring through the wire fence into the lens of the camera, emotionless and broken. Some of the pictures were of piles of bones and skulls. We've seen these pictures a million times, perhaps too many times.

But I didn't really get it, it all seemed too alien and otherworldly to properly grasp. They didn't horrify me; they were too far removed from anything I could understand. I didn't really have a context, and photographs are meaningless without context. Of course as I got older I learnt the context and learnt the horror.

It was hard to go to Germany without having all that stuff running through your head. On our first tour we all bought really cool German Army motorcycle boots. When a gang of you were clumping down the cobbles of Berlin's Waldemarstrasse at three in the morning, when everything else was silent, you couldn't help but hear the echoes of darker times. But there were loads of other strong, more positive images of Germany in our heads at the same time. The modern Germany was at the forefront of Green Politics, it had a huge squatting movement, loads of interesting political groups, some fantastic ground breaking music (we were big fans of Can and Faust in particular), and loads of really cool, imaginative, arty, intelligent people. Not for nothing was Hamburg 'the cradle of British Rock'.

Being in Germany in 1980 was great; being in Berlin was something else.

Predictably we stayed in Kreuzburg, the squat capital of the world at that moment. Kreuzburg is right by the wall, a big Turkish area. It was also home to a very large community of squatters, anarchists, Hell's Angels, Gay Libbers, Environmentalists, artists, bands, and freaks of all persuasion. Berlin was teeming with young people. One of the reasons for this was because Germans who lived in Berlin didn't have to go into the army. Conscription was still in place in Germany then. Moving to Berlin was a way of avoiding it.

It wasn't just that though. It attracted people due to it's peculiar and unique psycho-geography. No other place existed in the same situation. It was very weird for us, and it was probably just as weird for everybody else. A walled, land-locked city of politics and partying; surrounded by a monolithic, mysterious, authoritarian regime that kept its people in by force. A regime that, we were told, wanted to destroy our way of life. That wanted to subject us to a jack-booted, dictatorial order, watched over by secret police and government agents, where any misdemeanours or indiscretions would be punished mercilessly, possibly in some hard-labour camp. A place where every move was watched, every relationship scrutinised, and every act regarded with suspicion. I don't know if the East was really like that, but that is what we were brought up to believe. Not only were we at cold-war with these neighbours, but the attendant nuclear arms race between the two systems added an extra element of danger to the mix. The contrast between the youth culture of West Berlin and the perceived culture of East Germany made it a potent, creative and vibrant, psychic space. So different from anything else I had experienced, but then, I wasn't very experienced.

We stayed in a huge factory, which had been turned into a commune. The main guy we dealt with was called Karl, and he had big, heavy, dark, painted eyebrows. A powerful guy with a fund of stories about actions and riots and the sort of stuff that used to impress us in those days. The squat was a model of efficiency and togetherness, but also a lot of fun. I think a lot of English people don't get that about the Germans. The stereotype is of an efficient, well organised, intelligent and serious people, but with little sense of humour. I have never felt this to be the case. While, generally, the former part of the statement is true, the second is completely wide of the mark. Every time I go to Germany I meet really funny, witty, erudite men and women who have a lot of fun, a lot of laughs, and a tremendous enthusiasm for life. I would happily live there.

When we arrived at the squat in Kreuzburg, the first thing we did was to ask how to get dope. Karl passed us a large supermarket style, plastic carrier bag. It was of full of grass. As we left a few days later, we handed back the bag, now completely empty save for a sad and small collection of seeds and stems. Karl was slightly crest fallen, he informed us, "that bag of grass would have lasted this commune a whole year, you have smoked it in less than a week!"

We use to go up on the roof of the building, get wrecked and signal across the wall with a torch. There were probably all sorts of insurrectionary actions and plotting going on in the squats and streets below, but you could always count on Zounds to be up on the roof smoking dope and discussing the lives everyone else are living.

Clash City mockers

We went back to Berlin for a couple of gigs in May 1981, where we were afforded a glimpse of the flip side of the punk coin. The Clash were in town on their German tour, playing at The Eissporthalle. This was something akin to the Wembley Arena, vast, impersonal, soulless and functional. We decided to go to the venue the day of the gig to try to meet up with our punk brothers and get on the guest list for the gig. We drove across Berlin to the venue and walked around it until we found a way in. We could hear the unmistakable sound of the Clash going through their paces inside. We got in at the back of the venue and looked across the empty arena at the band sound-checking on stage. Sounded fantastic. Thundering rhythm, great guitar and Joe barking out 'White Riot' or whatever

87

it was. We walked up to the stage and as we got nearer something seemed weird. We could hear the authentic sound of The Clash, but the musicians playing and singing were people we had never seen before. Very confusing. When they finished we approached them and explained who we were and why we were there. They explained that The Clash never did their own sound checks, the roadies did them. To be honest they could have done the gigs for them as well. There was no difference.

The roadies told us where the band were staying and we drove over there. In contrast to our own situation they were staying at a five star, luxury hotel. Punk rock eh lads? As we pulled up they were coming out of the door. We ran over to them. They spotted us and froze. They looked coked up and nervous, maybe they thought we were going to attack them. Anyway, we explained again who we were and they relaxed a bit and said they would arrange tickets for their gig that night.

When we turned up at the gig it was the typical, unpleasant, big arena type vibe. There were police everywhere, with vicious Dobermans barking and frothing and straining at the leash. We went round to the stage door. No tickets had been arranged for us and no one seemed to know who we were. We talked our way in anyway and sat back to watch the gig. They were really good, but no better, or different, to the band of roadies that did the sound check. The Clash didn't seem to be having anywhere near as much fun as we were having. I'm sure they would have had a much groovier time if they'd been staying in the squats with us. I felt a bit sorry for them.

18 TRUE LOVE

I hit the button on the radio
I hear yet another song about
True love I wonder what it's all about
I'd like to taste a little bit of that
Don't know if I've ever encountered it
It seems to hang so many people up
Sweet dreams are something that I never get
True love what's it really all about

Every newspaper that I pick up
Has some way to help me in my search
New shoes or maybe a new pair of jeans
Got to find a way to sell myself
One girl for every boy that wanted one
One boy, that's the way it's always been
Watch out if that's not how it is for you
Some folks they find it hard to handle that

Boy meets girl and girl meets boy
Live through pain and tears and joy
But that's not how it looks to me
It looks just like a drag to me

Sometimes it seems just like a joke to me
Reading in someone's glossy magazines
About a love that is a special thing
Ends up with someone's arms in someone's sink
Look twice, it's not such a funny thing
Not just hearts and songs and wedding rings
Can be a whole lot of different things
Can be pettiness and jealousy

True love - what's it really all about

True Love

"Three and a half million children are being brought up by single parents, 90% by their mothers"
The World Tonight BBC Radio 4 – 13.01.11

I was at school from 1961 until 1972. In all the time I was there I never once heard of another child in my situation. That is, with divorced parents, living with their grandparents and sharing a bedroom with their uncle. My grandparents provided me with asylum, but it still made me feel like a freak.

It led to me becoming very cynical about the institution of marriage; the notion of romantic love, and it opened my eyes to the violence and aggression that can lurk not very far beneath the surface of those things.

Years later in the 1970s and 80s thousands of young people, including Zounds and their peers and associates, started to live collectively and to question everything they had been told. This wasn't without historical precedent, it was happening as far back as the Diggers in the seventeenth century, but it seemed new and revolutionary to us.

Issues around possessive love, sexual jealousy, sexuality, polymorphous perversity, child rearing and all other aspects of human relationships were questioned and explored. All under the spotlight and glare of feminism and the women's movement.

There were a lot of Lesbian, separatist houses around our squats in Brougham Road, and it helped to intensify an atmosphere where all the old power relations and certainties were examined and deconstructed.

The women we were living with and around were strong, liberated individuals who helped shape the scene and the agenda as much as the boys in the bands. And, though the post punk scene meant there were loads more women doing music on their own terms, it was still overwhelmingly male, masculine and a bit of a boys club.

But then why wouldn't it be? Rock n roll is the product of a patriarchal system that privileges males. If there is any money, reputation or kudos to be made from it, it is of course going to go overwhelmingly to men.

19 MORE TROUBLE COMING EVERY DAY

You're in the living room you're painting your nails
Your mother says where did we go wrong
Your father says don't be late home tonight
Your brother wants you to get off the phone
The same old things everyday
The same old things the same old people say
How much longer must it go on this way
It looks as though nothing's ever gonna change

And it's just more trouble coming everyday
It's just more trouble coming everyday
And if things don't change I bet you'll scream
And then they'll just get worse
More Trouble Coming Everyday

You'd go out dancing but the clubs are full
Of people getting ready to fight
What's more none of your friends
Are allowed to go down town tonight
The smell of burning gives you such a thrill
Out with the old and in with the new
You don't wanna see anyone hurt
But you just gotta get out of this place

And it's just more trouble coming everyday
It's just more trouble coming everyday
And if things don't change I bet you'll scream
And then they'll just get worse
More Trouble Coming Everyday

Here it comes, here it comes, here it comes
Here it comes, here it comes, here it comes

More Trouble Coming Every Day

Inner city riots – White n-words – Zappa again – I'm a girl

I wrote this song in 1981 when Bristol, Brixton, Birmingham and loads of other places, not necessarily beginning with B, were the scenes of widespread, inner city rioting. These places were decaying and moribund as manufacturing industry collapsed, old industries withered away, unemployment rose and Britain's Empire dream was eventually consigned to the shredder of history.

The grim futility of a 'futureless future' consisting of a shabby, hand to mouth existence in a crumbling, post industrial hinterland, with no prospect of improvement, led to a generation that felt embittered and dispossessed. Not only were we expected to live in these conditions, but also to suffer the perpetual harassment of a police force that seemed to see everyone else as the 'enemy'. This was all much worse for black people. When we were living in places without a large black population we use to get stopped and hassled all the time by the police. When we moved to London I noticed we were mostly left alone by the cops, because they were too busy hassling black people. Now there was someone else lower down the ladder than us.

The squatter, punk, bohemia scene wasn't particularly multi-racial. Maybe a bit more when the 2 Tone thing happened, but generally the black scene was quite separate. You always noticed it if there was a black person at a gig. Even though lots of white kids were into reggae and dub, you tended to see it in separate venues, colleges mainly. When we saw Linton Kwesi Johnson at the Marquee, it was all white people in the audience. The same with Steel Pulse and Aswad. A lot of white kids would not have gone to Reggae venues like the 4 Aces in Dalston. Largely it was, as filmmaker Isaac Julien describes, separate 'territories'.

The riots brought a lot of people out on the streets. While black people might be getting the worst of it, the white working class kids were getting it too. The anger might not have been very focused, but it could no longer be contained.

That was what the song 'More Trouble Coming Every Day' was supposed to be about. It was meant to be an update of the themes covered by Frank Zappa in his song 'Trouble Coming Every Day', which he wrote about the 1966 'race riots' in Watts, Los Angeles. But my song turned out to be much more mundane than that. The message is referred to so obliquely it is barely noticeable. The only hint of it really is in the last lines

'The smell of burning gives you such a thrill, out with the old and in with the new, you don't wanna see anyone hurt, but you just gotta get out of this place'.

Essentially I had written another whiny song about discontented teenagers. The song was a failure on another level as well. In an attempt to break away from gender typing I wanted to write the song from a female perspective, in a first person narrative, as a girl. I don't know what happened there because afterwards I realised I'd just written another third person story about, not by, a girl. Not very groundbreaking.

20 KNIFE

I can look in the mirror and not recognise
The reflection that is appearing on the other side
I know that hat and that coat that shirt and that tie
But I can't seem to remember who's been living inside

Sometimes I think I'll go and get a knife
And cut all of my clothes down into rags
Sometimes I think I'll take a holiday
From wearing my opinions like a badge

I've been down on the pavement I've been shopping for
clothes
But it's just one uniform then another all standing in
rows
A new outfit a new outlook another show
I shed one skin from my body then another one grows

Sometimes I think I'll go and get a knife
And cut all of my clothes down into rags
Sometimes I think I'll take a holiday
From wearing my opinions like a badge

Knife

Making records

This was the last thing we did in the early period. It's the most musically sophisticated record and very atmospheric. Tim Hutton was really present on this track, with his strong bass line, cool backing vocals, and even playing the trumpet. No wonder he went on to arrange for Ian Browne and a host of other pop stars. Brian Pugsley played keyboards, he went on to produce the Shamen and Bjork. So it is just me then, living the life of a homeless has-been and selling the Big Issue.

To me records and live performances are completely different things. They are separate mediums, and I like to treat them differently. You can make some great records by just playing live in the studio. But it will never be like playing live at a gig. At a gig you have all the atmosphere of immediacy, the 'liveness', the possibility that it could all go dreadfully wrong, or incredibly right. It is exciting because it is uncertain. But you can never get that on a record. So you have to do something else. Zounds always wanted to be a bit more expansive on records. We didn't ever just go in and lay down the live thing and leave it at that. Of course we thought The Ramones first album was brilliant, but The Beach Boys' Pet Sounds is brilliant too. Not that I'm saying Zounds were in the same league as either The Ramones or The Beach Boys

There is no right way to do it. But we were imaginative people and wanted the chance to use our imagination. And of course, when you are heavy dope smokers in an environment with big speakers and machines for making weird noises, you can't help but get carried away.

It's a real fucking mystery as to what makes a good record, it's not even about whether it's a good or bad song. The same song can be done a million ways. Great songs can make terrible records and inconsequential songs can make great records. It is not easy to make a good record. It is the most mysterious art. I have always wanted to make really great records, but it is a constant state of disappointment realising that I can't. But then most people can't. The only one I made that even came close to being any good was Demystification. Why it worked I don't know. Just something about the playing, the singing, the atmosphere, the constant reverb that goes on throughout it. If I could get that sound again I would, but I just don't know how it happened.

Zounds fell into a weird situation that we couldn't break out of. Because of our association with Crass and our general stance on things a lot of people were put off of listening to us. I think they expected the usual old 500 miles-per-hour-punk-schlock-driller-killer-sexless-blur. That wasn't us at all. Some of the people who were attracted to the image found the music a bit poppy and wimpy, so it was ever diminishing returns all round. I always thought it strange how so many people who described themselves as anarchists could be so closed minded and so stuck in such a narrow rut. Especially as it was such an unoriginal rut.

You can hear the dissatisfaction with the whole youth, uniform thing in the lyrics to Knife. While it's a generalised comment on fashion, image and identity, it's also a bit of a dig at some of the audience, and it's never a good idea to offend the audience, because then they don't buy your records. The strange thing is, we are a lot more popular now, and a lot better known than we ever were before. I've even got to quite like Zounds myself.

21 NOT ME

Who is gonna be one of the crowd
Who is gonna be there shouting out loud
Who is gonna be hanging around
Cheering at a flag, someone's waving around

Not me - Not me - Not me - Not me
Not me - Not me - Not me - Not me

Who is gonna be one of the herd
Sitting and standing at somebody's word
Who is gonna be down in the square
Just cause someone else says you better be there

Not me - Not me - Not me - Not me
Not me - Not me - Not me - Not me

Who is gonna be one of the crowd
Sitting and standing and shouting out loud
Who is gonna be lead round on a string
Thinking what someone else told them to think

Not me - Not me - Not me - Not me
Not me - Not me - Not me - Not me

22 BIAFRA

Black were the people in the country of Biafra
On the continent of Africa, where the sun beat down like
fire
The people and their babies had teeth and mouths and
bellies
Like all people on the planet it was food that fuelled
their bellies

They worked and farmed and traded so that not a mouth went
empty
For everyone was plenty when the wealth was shared out
fairly
They were diligent and peaceful, quiet, content,
resourceful
Like all the people on the planet they had a fate most
foul and dreadful

And black is the petrol that flows around in engines
Transports us very quickly to another destination
It's important, it is vital, it's the drug and we're the
addicts
More and more and more must come to satisfy the habit

Now people of the kingdom that have lakes of oil beneath
them
If you look on maps of Africa you won't find Biafra on
them
People of the kingdom that have lakes of oil beneath them
If you look on maps of Africa you won't find Biafra on
them

23 WOLVES

Oh come and listen my darling daughter
Don't step outside the house tonight
We're safe in here the bolts are fastened
The windows shuttered secure and tight
When daytime comes we can go out walking
Run and play till the sun goes down
But when darkness falls we must stay well hidden
Our enemies might come to town.
Daddy's got a good job he's working for a bank
Investing lots of money into aeroplanes and tanks
There are other people that just don't understand
Daddy needs the money and must make all that he can
Working yes he's working and he loves the company
His profit is another's loss another's misery
All those other people they've got no house to live
Why should daddy worry and think he has to give
To those silly, lazy people who sit and waste their time
Complaining about daddy and the people daddy likes
I'm his pretty daughter and I know he loves me
He buys us lots of things just so that everyone can see
We go in every evening and pull the shutters down
Daddy just gets worried that the wolves might come to
town.
Come and listen my darling son
All I've built could come undone
If the people that live outside of town
Decide to come and shoot us down.
They come into the town like packs of wolves
They see in the dark, they see in the dark
They don't have any fear for themselves
Take a chance, take a chance
Into the town, starting to prowl
Looking for us, people like us
We're just lucky people who've got what we deserve
Why should we pay, why should we pay
To the likes of them and their brutal ways
It's not fair baby it's not fair
Into the town starting to prowl
Looking for us baby people like us
We're just lucky people who've got what we deserve

Why should we pay, why should we pay
To the likes of them and their brutal ways
It's not fair baby it's not fair
Into the town, starting to prowl
If we could catch them we would kill them.
Come and listen my darling daddy
Your son went out after dark
The note I found in the car this morning
Said I've joined the wolves and the wolves will bark

La vache qui rit

The decline and fall of Zounds - On tour in England and
Scotland - Line up changes - The last European gigs –
It was all just too medieval - Kurt Vonnegut –
Bob Marley dies in Hanover

Trouble on tour

By the time of our last European tour in early 1982 it was no fun anymore.

Prior to going to Europe we had toured Britain. It had been somewhat edgy and the mood in the country was becoming more desperate. For me the 1980s were the worst decade in the history of the world. The chill winds of historic change were starting to blow up a storm and it was making people harder and more uncompromising. The cold war was hotting up, the Falklands war and miners strike were just around the corner, the poll tax and clause 28 were gestating. Everybody could see the way it was going, it wasn't pretty, and people get jumpy when the whip starts to come down.

We played Huddersfield Polytechnic and there was a riot. The Poly rugby club had been hired as security and refused entrance to all the local punk rockers because they were not students. The punks stormed the door and it all went off. This made us nervous because shortly before that we had played the Bentley Pavilion in Doncaster. Some local beer monsters stormed the venue after the gig had finished and a huge fight had broken out. Laurence got badly beaten up and was hospitalised. I hid in a corner wielding my bass like an axe and trying not to cry.

Between Doncaster and Huddersfield we went to Scotland. In Aberdeen the support band were booed off and some microphones were stolen. The crowd were glued up and particularly out of it. Foregoing my personal safety I strode out on to the stage like some latter day Spartacus and demanded the return of the microphones, informing the baying audience that we could not play with out them.

There was a lot of shouting and barracking and I wasn't sure if it was supportive or hostile. I started to worry that this little scenario might not play out as well as I had hoped. Eventually a sheepish looking boy-punk came up and gave us back the mics. He was cheered to the rafters for his heroic act of generosity, despite the fact he was the thieving toe-rag that had stolen them in the first place, and in the process jeopardised the gig from going ahead. It did turn out to be a fantastic night though.

The audience went crazy and had a lot of fun, but they were quite sad and desperate actually. It had been two years since the election of Thatcher and things were biting harder much earlier up in the North of Scotland. Mass unemployment was becoming a way of life. Some of the kids at the Aberdeen gig were hassling us to take them to London so they could work as roadies for us. They didn't realise we were all on the dole as well.

I think a lot of people get the impression that because a band has records in the independent charts, is touring foreign countries, and being featured in the music press, that they must have two halfpennies to rub together. Not Zounds. It might be different for other bands but we were pioneering the D.I.Y. scene, which meant endless benefits for lost causes or fake causes. Over the years I have come to realise that a lot of money is made in the music-biz, but musicians don't get any of it.

By that stage in the band's life most of the gigs we were playing were organised by fans and didn't pay well, if at all. Why should people pay for musicians to eat when the off-licences still had cider on the shelves? Logic told them that the more cider they drank, the closer the world would come to the glory-day when anarchy, peace and endless free alcohol would replace work, war and boredom as the main features of everyday life. A sort of down-market, crusty take on Big Rock Candy Mountain.

After Aberdeen we played Dundee where there was a gang of National Front skinheads sieg-heiling along to the music. Terrifying. At the time Dundee had more gangs then anywhere in Europe. We were put up on a grim council housing estate where all the shops had been closed down and boarded up due to perpetual break-ins and vandalism. They had mobile shops that came round a few times a day, like ice cream vans.

Touring was becoming a drag. Relationships in the band were strained and we were becoming directionless. Things had got a bit complex and gone sour in Brougham Road too. I moved out. Friendships were breaking down, both in the band and in our personal lives. Musical differences were coming to the fore. It seemed to be cold all the time. It's one thing to hold notions of freedom intellectually, but to be able to cope with them emotionally, in a cold, hard world is a different matter. Added to all this, my girlfriend was pregnant and everybody was running around with everybody else, very confusing. Ego, sexual jealousy, possessiveness, status, belonging; all these complex issues are present in any group of people. But when you are living closely, in a communal situation, where there are no boundaries between work, play and home, then those notions come even more sharply into focus. I don't know about anybody else, but I was fucked up, I couldn't handle stuff, I was a mess. And 'La Vache Qui Rit' is a complete mess.

A benefit for someone and a new line up

The record started out full of hope and optimism though. The original intention was that it was to be a benefit release for an anti-military, anti-draft organisation in Belgium. It was also supposed to be a double header with us on one side and the Mob on the other. The Mob were going to do a version of 'No Doves Fly Here' in French. Classy band.

Joseph, Laurence and I set out for Belgium and recorded 'Biafra' and 'Not Me' in a rudimentary four-track demo studio outside of Brussels. It wasn't really the kind of studio we were used to. With Crass Records and Rough Trade we recorded in good, professional studios with experienced engineers who were used to making proper records that would be played on the radio. Records made to a technical specification that meant they could at least be played up against commercially released records and not sound, weedy or amateurish. The place we were using for this recording was the sort of makeshift, homemade set up that we thought we had left behind. You can hear the difference between it and the rest of our output. Why we did it I don't know. The Mob were a bit cannier and never recorded their side of the E.P.

We had a nice time though, as the whole thing was being put together by Phil The Terrible, who like Geoff Travis, is another of the decent people in the music industry. We did a few gigs with the Mob who were on tour there, and then we came home.

But things started to go wrong after that. We had already had problems recording 'Dancing' and 'True Love'. Joseph hated what we were doing and walked out of the sessions. Tim Hutton, who was drumming with the Mob at that time, was visiting us in the studio, so he played drums on those tracks. He was great, a very powerful drummer and a very sophisticated musician.

Things were changing fast though. Joseph was unhappy with Laurence's guitar playing and felt my more direct, rudimentary approach would solidify the sound a bit, make it fuller and less fussy. He suggested I move over to rhythm guitar and we get Tim in on bass. So Tim joined Zounds on bass and left the Mob. Then Joseph joined the Mob on drums so he was playing with both bands. There were some gigs where none of the other bands would bring a drummer, so Joseph would play all night with 3 or 4 different groups. By the time he played with us he would be knackered and not up to it.

The line up of Lake, Wood, Porter and Hutton then recorded the last single 'More Trouble Coming Every Day' and 'Knife', though that was released before 'La Vache Qui Rit'.

Wolves

This was recorded in Leiden on the last European tour with the Steve/Laurence/Joseph/Tim line up, along with a not very good version of Fear. 'Wolves' was an older song that we re-introduced at Tim's request. I didn't really like it. I had written it with previous guitarist Nick and we dropped it from the set as soon as he left the band. I would never have chosen to put it on a record, and it gave Nick even more ammunition to fuel his hatred of me, and his assertion that we ripped him off.

That last European adventure was a weird tour (again). A load of friends from Brougham Road turned up when we played in Antwerp, which was the party capital of Europe at that time. After the gig we stayed in some sort of medieval tower that was the home of a psychologically challenging, ex-prostitute the Mob had introduced us to. A load of us were hanging out in this tower when someone brought a message that Tim had been arrested in a club for not having any ID. Most of the party decided they would go to the police station with the passport and rescue him.

I would never go to a police station willingly so I stayed put with Max, the enigmatic, delightful and 'out of it' roadie we had borrowed from The Mob. For some reason I put on Nico's 'Marble Index'. The deathly, Teutonic 'Dietrich on heroin' vocals, the morbid, droney harmonium, and John Cale's dense, other worldy arrangements, seemed to be emanating from the very walls of the tower. I think I was in danger of losing it. The abyss was opening up and Nico and Cale weren't making it any easier. Then the door to the room crashed open and Tim, with two armed cops gripping his arms, exploded into the room. Tim was shouting 'I've been arrested, they chucked me in the van and wouldn't let me take a piss. I've pissed myself, look I'm soaked, where's my passport?' 'The others have taken it to the police station,' I replied, while surreptitiously trying to hide the dope. I was no longer sure if we were in Belgium or Holland, whether the stuff was illegal or not. Without a word, the police turned and dragged Tim back out of the room, shouting and kicking. They had come and gone like a poltergeist; disruptive, noisy, and furious. It was so unexpected it was hard to know whether it had really happened or not. Max and I and sat, staring silently at each other, totally bewildered, stoned, unnerved and exhausted. And still Nico droned on, magnificently, monotonously and mesmerisingly, into the weird, medieval night.

Eventually everyone returned for a night of further weirdness and psychic terrorism on the part of our confrontational hostess. She was seriously into fucking up our heads and seemed to know all the right buttons to press.

It was on that tour that Laurence suggested we break up the band and start something new when we got back home. I agreed. I have a policy of never regretting anything, but I do have some regret for agreeing to that. I should have told Laurence to leave at that point and got some one else in. But I was about to enter a period of being completely lost musically. For years and years after that I had no confidence and let myself be controlled by other people, I made a few bad records and no good ones in the process.

We got back home and there was a messy and acrimonious

dissolution of the band. We cancelled the last couple of gigs in the date sheet and that was it for quite a while. I told Phil of Not So Brave he could do what he liked with the 'La Vache Qui Rit' record. I had had enough and just didn't care any more. The Mob had pulled out of doing the record, the benefit aspect of it disappeared, and Phil chose the tracks. The two we recorded in the demo studio 'Biafra' and 'Not Me', and the two live ones from Leiden. I just didn't care. I had so many hang ups and problems in my personal life that I just wanted to leave the whole scene, change my life and try to enter the mainstream for a bit. I was about to spin out of control and needed a bit of grounding in 'ordinary life'. Of course that can drive you mad as well, which it did eventually.

Joseph carried on playing in The Mob and then his own band Blyth Power. Tim went on to arrange for, and play with, a succession of genuine pop chart stars and Laurence became an accomplished video editor. I got a job and continued playing with local loser bands that were never going anywhere.

Biafra

THERE is a "Kingdom of Biafra" on some old maps which were made by early white explorers of the west coast of Africa. Nobody is now sure what that kingdom was, what its laws and arts and tools were like. No tales survive of the kings and queens. As for the "Republic of Biafra" we know a great deal. It was a nation with more citizens than Ireland and Norway combined. It proclaimed itself an independent republic on May 30, 1967. On January 17 of 1970, it surrendered unconditionally to Nigeria, the nation from which it had tried to secede. It had few friends in this world, and among its active enemies were Russia and Great Britain. Its enemies were pleased to call it a "tribe." **KV**

I formulated the idea for this song in Hanover during a short German tour in 1981. It's not even my idea, it is just a précis of **Biafra: A People Betrayed - by Kurt Vonnegut**, an article he wrote on returning from the warzone there.

My main aim will not be to move readers to voluptuous tears with tales about innocent black children dying like flies, about rape and looting and murder and all that. I will tell instead about an admirable nation that lived for less than three years. De mortuis nil nisi bonum. Say nothing but good of the dead. **KV**

It resonated with me because there was a period when I was a kid when the news was full of images of grotesque, pot bellied, fly covered, malnourished children and adults. And these were called Biafrans. No one knew where the fuck Biafra was, no one knew what was going on there or why. No one knew anything when I was a kid, not in Reading anyway. What's more, nobody seemed to want to know anything. All I knew was that in the child-world I inhabited, Biafran became a term of derision and abuse aimed at skinny people. I don't know why people idealise and romanticise the 'innocence of children'. My memory and observations have led me to believe there is a cruel and malicious streak running deep in the veins of the western child.

*We flew over water, there were Russian trawlers below. They were monitoring every plane that came into Biafra. The Russians were helpful in a lot of ways: They gave the Nigerians Ilyushin bombers and MIGs and heavy artillery. And the British gave the Nigerians artillery too and advisers, and tanks and armored cars, and machine guns and mortars and all that, and endless ammunition. **KV***

Vonnegut wanted to tell the story of the great aspects of Biafran culture and society, something positive and uplifting. He didn't want to wallow in their destruction and suffering, so I wanted to mirror that and have music that was very up. What is more life affirming and groovy and primal than the Bo Diddley beat? Especially when combined with the chords from Elvis Presley's 'His Latest Flame'.

*And the officer who showed us around, also a graduate of Sandhurst, said, "There wouldn't be all this fuss, you know, if it weren't for the petroleum." He was speaking of the vast oil field beneath our feet. We asked him who owned the oil, and I expected him to say ringingly that it was the property of the Biafran people now. But he didn't. "We never nationalized it," he said. "It still belongs to British Petroleum and Shell." He wasn't bitter. I never met a bitter Biafran. **KV***

The last part of the song crashes into a doomy minor key section as the destruction of Biafra is eventually confronted and contrasted with the preceding verses.

I have written all this quickly. I find that I have betrayed my promise to speak of the greatness rather than the pitifulness of the Biafran people. I have mourned the children copiously. I have told of *a woman who was drenched in gasoline. **KV***

I agree with Kurt Vonnegut, whatever the tragedies we face, it is important to hang on to the great stuff too, otherwise what's the point? We might as well chuck it all in now.

*Some wonder whether they, in order to be up to date, should hate Nigerians now. I tell them, "no." **KV***

Bob Marley died that day

I conceived the song 'Biafra' on the day of a gig in Hanover. We weren't introduced to the audience at the start of the show so when we stepped out to play I rushed to the microphone and screamed out 'Ladies and gentleman, all the way from Trenchtown, Kingston, Jamaica, Bob Marley and the Wailers!" Then we roared into the first number. The next day, coming down to one of those excellent German breakfasts, our hosts informed us that Bob Marley died in the night. A coincidence that had us smoking much grass and playing football to the memory of Bob.

24 ALONE

In every corner a hostile face
A house divided is a lonely place
Your body stiffens your heart starts to race
Does everyone else here feel so alone

You're alone in your private world
Turning into a private hell
Being treated in a private ward

In every window a silhouette
Ten million people I've never met
Ten million stories its not over yet
Tear down the walls lets stop being alone

You're alone in your private world
Turning into a private hell
Being treated in a private ward

A child is running through the city at night
Caught in the glare of the big store lights
Promises much but delivers little
You're still hurt trapped in the
middle
Blown by the wind and pushed by the dollar
Addicted to the glamour and the glitter
And the squalor
Your fate is decided by the flip of a coin
Is it any wonder you feel so alone?

In every corner a hostile face
A house divided is a lonely place
Your body stiffens your heart starts to race
Does everyone else here feel so alone

You're alone in your private world
Turning into a private hell
Being treated in a private ward

Alone

Zounds from beyond the grave - Father Raymond - Vi Subversa - Disgraced in Blackpool - Redemption through McLibel

Over the years there were a number of reunions of the Curse of Zounds line up. On 14th November 1992 we played at a birthday benefit party for a friend of Joseph's called Father Raymond. He was an ex Benedictine Monk from Rumania. He escaped to England and followed The Mob and Blyth Power around the country. I may have the specifics slightly wrong here but it was something of that order. At the time I was in my fat-Elvis period and going mental. I stayed like that for quite a few years. We also played at Vi Subversa's birthday bash at the Astoria on 3rd June 1995. A lovely gig and so good to see the Poison Girls again. Sadly they have been partially written out of the anarcho story, not that they will give a fuck about that.

On the 11th August 1996 Joseph also got us a gig at the first 'Holidays In The Sun' at Blackpool (now known as Rebellion). Joseph wasn't in great financial shape at the time and we were offered an unfeasible £1500 to play. We played the gig and managed to alienate a number of supporters of the band who thought it was a commercial rip-off event. We played dreadfully, disappointing a number of fans who turned up to see us. Then we got ripped off when the promoter said he had run out of money and couldn't pay any of the bands playing on the Sunday. That pretty much sums up Zounds really.

We got together again to play a couple of benefit gigs and record a benefit single for the McLibel campaign. In 1990 the McDonald's corporation sued Dave Morris and Helen Steel for publishing and distributing leaflets highlighting some facts about McDonalds's activities. It was the longest trial in world legal history, and it cost McDonald's millions of dollars. Hurray! I spoke to Jon Active, who was one of the organisers of the campaign, and asked if we could to do something to help.

As I had known Dave for years this was one benefit I was actually happy to be involved in. Dave had been a regular visitor to Debby Webb's place, where Zounds had disgraced themselves by not paying the phone bill when organising the second Weird Tales tour. Dave also let me take over his squat in Brougham Road when he left to ferment insurrection around the globe. In a way it was Dave who facilitated the whole Brougham Road anarcho, punk, scene by bequeathing me his squat. We did two fantastic gigs on 13th and 14th September 1997 at Hackney's Chat's Palace. We also recorded a single that included an epic remake of 'This Land', backed with an old/new song we had never previously finished, 'Alone'.

In 1998 we did another McLibel gig at ULU in central London, which I thought was fantastic, but Laurence hated. He said his playing was out of tune and terrible. I thought it was better than he usually managed. The gig was mainly memorable though for its Spinal Tap finale where we got lost in the back stage tunnels. We stumbled around for about 15 minutes and eventually came up in the dressing room. But Laurence wasn't with us. We made a few frantic calls and finally tracked him down a couple of hours later at his house. While lost in the tunnels he found a fire exit and slipped out unnoticed, as he was embarrassed about his playing.

After every gig, I always claimed it would be the last one. No more Zounds. Now I take the opposite view and will never disband Zounds again. What's the point? I would just have to find something else to do and I haven't got that much imagination.

25 GO ALL THE WAY FOR THE USA

This is the part, the part where I say
Would you go all the way for the USA
Over the top at the end of the day
Would you go all the way for the USA
Would you do it for Disney, do it for Nixon
Do it for Hoover, donner and blitzen
Would you do it for Lockheed, for Smith and for Wesson
Do it for Florida and southern elections

This is the part, the part where I say
Would you go all the way for the USA
Would you go all the way for the CIA
Would you go all the way for the NRA
Would you go all the way for MTV
Would you go all the way for KFC
Would you do it for Enron, do it for Exxon
Would you do it for WorldCom, for Smith and for Wesson

Welcome to the world of paradise lost
Everything has its price and we're counting the cost

Would you go all the way for the USA
Do you wanna die for the USA
Do you wanna kill for the USA
Would you go all the way for the USA

26 WAR FEVER

A will to war
A war to will
To kill for more
More blood to spill
Spill into war
A clash of wills
The will to force
To force the will
Caesar reigns
Over us all
His feet and crown
Anoint with oil
The senators
To share the spoils
The usurers
Finance it all

27 KAMP AMERICA

Fifteen years of schooling and they put you on the night
shift
Grinning like an idiot seven to eleven
Then they train you like a monkey and they put you in the
zoo
Won't you have a nice day like they ordered you to
Someone's putting something in your pretty little head
Dancing on your grave like you're already dead
They're singing like a siren and you give a little purr
Fifteen years of schooling and the only thing you're
saying
As you're looking for a way out as you're looking for
escape
Would you like fries with that sir

From Azerbaijan to Reykjavik
The South China Sea to the South Pacific
From the Great Gates of Kiev to the Berlin Zoo
From Regents Park to Waterloo

We're all living in Kamp Amerika now
We're all working for Kamp Amerika now
We're all equal in Kamp Amerika now
We're all living in Kamp Amerika now

From the Hollywood Hills in Los Angeles
To the real live wires of New York's Wall Street
All over the world to every town
American Caesar sending his boys round

Go All The Way

2002 – 2005 - Protag & Stick - Colchester Steve - Punk rock in the Balkans - Biblical riots in Thessaloniki - Trouble on the border - Pack it in lads

I reformulated Zounds in 2002 as the build up to the US war on Iraq intensified and the post 9/11 world shape-shifted. Old alliances fractured and new enmities came to the fore. In the new world I felt more connected to Zounds again. I felt closer to the music and the spirit. Not that Zounds is about international politics, but the external, macrocosmic world is always intimately connected with the world of soul. Also I got an electric guitar and amplifier for the first time in years and really felt the desire to play it very loud.

Eventually war broke out in Iraq on 20th March 2003 and I watched it unfold on television. As I did so I wrote a set of songs for an album called 'The Wounds Of Zounds'. We recorded it but I never let it be released. It was OK but it wasn't really good enough. I salvaged 3 songs for a CD E.P. and brought it out as a limited edition.

I didn't want anyone from previous line-ups in the band, and none of them were available anyway. I got Protag in because he could play bass and he was a part of the Zounds family. He also had the right outlook and is a very funny, perceptive, selfless and kind person. His first band, The Instant Automatons, had done gigs with Zounds in our early days and were connected to the Fuck Off records 'bad music scene'. He had then been in Joseph Porter's band Blyth Power for years. He'd also played in ATV for a while. Protag is one of the world's great people and is a mainstay of the 1 In 12 Club in Bradford. Protag brought Stick with him, a powerhouse drummer who had been a key member of Doom. He had also served time in Extreme Noise Terror, playing with Bill Drummond and KLF at their 'Brits Award' performance.

This was a rough and ready version of the band, and at that point my guitar playing was pretty ropey. We spent nearly 3 years touring around Europe. Some of the gigs were dynamite, others were so ramshackle that there are places where Zounds reputation is trashed forever.

Goodnight Vienna 2005

We stumbled along recording and gigging until 2005 when we undertook a long, arduous, band-breaking tour that took us down through the Balkans and back again. It's hard to go into the details of these things without dragging up a lot of painful, personal stuff that people probably don't want to be reminded of. Especially in the cold light of the printed page (or even the ghostly, hallucinatory flicker of the computer screen). Suffice to say, not everybody got on, and the spirit of Spinal Tap reared its ugly but truthful head once again, as it does on all tours by all bands. The best thing about it though was meeting 'Colchester Steve', who was getting a lift to London with Stick, Protag and Protag's girlfriend Anna (who had decided to come on the tour with us). Stick had a premonition that things might go wrong and that Colchester's presence would help soothe the situation. Luckily 'Colchester' had his passport on him and no fixed plans for the next three weeks, so he came. Stick was right, and when I collapsed in Stuttgart from physical, mental and emotional exhaustion, it was Colchester that carried me to safety and put me to bed. If he hadn't been there we might not have all lived to tell the tale.

After a few gigs in Northern Europe we headed down to Vienna where we played in a huge squatted building with it's own 'grand theatre'. During World War Two it had been the Headquarters of the 'Hitler Youth', and they had used the theatre to put on Nazi Party propaganda performances. It had a weird vibe, but not entirely negative, because it reminded you that even a regime as powerful, cruel and power-crazed as that, could be defeated and their places returned to the people.

But devastating news arrived just before we reached Vienna. Stick got a phone call from Bradford saying that his best friend Wayne, the singer with his band Doom, had died. Naturally Stick was distraught and started talking about leaving the tour. When? Now? Tomorrow? After the gig in Vienna? After a few days to go to the funeral? Suddenly everything was up in the air, and the tiredness and emotional burnout were only just beginning. The gig actually went really well. I was fired up at being able to sing songs like 'Dancing' and 'Great White Hunter' in a place that had been liberated from the most brutal regime in modern times. I was celebrating that. After the gig Colchester was sick and collapsed. I managed to get him to a bed and wondered how we were going to make it through the tour. We were less than a week into a three-week stint and people were dropping like flies. Stick decided to stay with the tour, but it was tough. And now the suppressed hostility between some members of the entourage was becoming open, and that can spread like the plague in such a confined and arduous situation.

Nothing is the same in the Balkans

We got to Serbia and it was a revelation to me. The infrastructure was crumbling, the roads were a mass of potholes, bumps and trenches. I just hadn't realised how poor and how neglected it was, like the third world in places. When we got to Belgrade, with its stereotypically Soviet-era, socialist style buildings, I thought I had been transplanted onto the pages of Orwell's 1984. There were cops everywhere you looked, nothing worked, people just looked poor and ground down. When we saw the wreckage of the twisted, bombed out television station, destroyed in a 1999 NATO air raid I really knew I was in a different place.

The first gig in Novi Sad was OK but nothing special. I was a bit nervous because when we walked on stage two Serbian giants dressed in classic, English, skinhead uniform started chanting fascist slogans and smashing glasses. A huge, fucking ruckus broke out and the audience turned on these people and beat the shit out of them. The skinheads staggered off saying they were coming back with their mates. One of the guys from the support band could see I was nervous and as soft as shit. He explained to me that it was the only language that sort understood and if they did bring their mates back, there were more than enough people at the gig to mete out more of the same. I'm not into violence, but I was glad the greater forces were on our side.

The next gig was in Belgrade the following night, and it turned out to be one of the best I have ever been involved in. Everything about the city was worn out, down at heel and generally fucked up. But the P.A. and the sound engineer were absolutely tremendous. And he got me incredibly stoned on some extremely high grade, Ukrainian pot. Loads of people had hired coaches to come to the gig from Hungary and Bulgaria. There was a real air of celebration at the event. Some of the people I spoke to told me how during the communist era they would get records by bands like Zounds, The Mob, Crass et al, sent to them from Western Europe, and how they would then be hauled into the police stations to explain why they were listening to these decadent, subversive, punk bands, and warned that their movements were being scrutinised by the security services. Jesus, I thought I was oppressed because W.H. Smiths wouldn't stock 'Anarchy In The UK'.

The gig was actually on the sixth anniversary of one of the most devastating NATO bombing raids on Belgrade. The atmosphere was highly charged, raucous, and excitable to a point I had never witnessed before. The commitment of the audience to just let go and scream and howl and give as much as the band, was an inspiration. It might have been the best gig I will ever do. In the middle of 'Target' is the chant

'You're welcome here Americans, we love you but not your bombs'.

The Serbians characterised the bombings in Belgrade as US bombing raids. When we did Target the intensity of feeling in the audience, and the energy and commitment with which they sang along to the chant was something I had never experienced before, either at a Zounds gig, or anywhere else. It may have been a ropey version of the band, but it was impossible not to rise to the occasion. Although the song was written about the introduction of cruise Missiles into Britain, making the UK a target for Eastern Bloc missiles, the song never ever had as much real meaning and resonance as it did when we played it that anniversary night in Belgrade.

We got back from the venue and Protag suffered some sort of breakdown. He just kept repeating, 'if my van breaks down I can fix it, if I breakdown no one can fix me'. We were staying on the sixteenth floor of a tower block and I suffered a prolonged anxiety attack as I just can't go that high. The support band had all been arrested for drunken driving on their way back to the flat. We slept for about two hours and then we had to do a massive drive down to Prilep in the south of Macedonia.

We got there really late. The gig was being put on by a group of fans from years ago. No body else knew who the fuck we were, but as only one other band had ever played in Prilep before it was a big event, and all the local kids turned up and went wild. The people we stayed with were lovely. They told us how poor the people were, and how, because of ancient rivalries with Greece, the country was suffering from lack of investment and was completely sidelined by the EU. Nothing in the country ran on legal software. Even the government was operating on pirated software, no one would sell them anything legal and at the time only six other countries recognised it as being an independent nation. They were getting no help from anyone and seemed to be a totally forgotten country.

The poverty was evident around Macedonia. People living in makeshift shelters under flyovers and bridges. People lining the roadside selling rubbish. At one point we threw some cardboard into a skip, and a woman climbed in to retrieve it. She then put it up for sale with her other bits of shit on the side of the road. I could not believe I was in Europe. By this point I was looking forward to getting to Greece. Getting back into the relative luxury of a modern EU country where it was once again the twentieth-first century. Parts of the Balkans didn't even seem to be twentieth-century, let alone twenty-first. Sadly I was in for another rude awakening.

Trouble on the Greek border

As we entered the customs post between Macedonia and Greece we handed all the passports to Protag's girlfriend Anna. There were two customs officials there, one in uniform, one in a beard, sunglasses and leather jacket, looking for all the world like an extra from 'Zorba The Greek'. The one not in uniform tried to take the passports, but Anna snatched them away and said she had no idea of this man's credentials, and she would only give them to the uniformed official. This went down very badly. They took us out of the van and searched us. They got a dog handler in to search the van. Everything was removed from the vehicle, the panels and fittings from the van were unscrewed and taken apart. The dog went into the van and found nothing. Then we saw the dog handler place a plastic bag under the seat and the dog found it. We had visions of rotting our lives away in a Greek jail. Stick was ready to kill Anna. In the end the dog handler, who had been conducting the search, told us nothing untoward had been found and we could reassemble the van, reload it, and be on our way. Then he said 'do it slowly, if you do it quick they will stop someone else and make me do this all over again and I will have to work late. If you take one hour then I will finish my shift and be able to go home to my dinner'. As we are obliging souls, even in the face of adversity, we complied with his wishes and then drove to the gig in Thessaloniki.

Biblical hoards and burning cars - I love the smell of teargas in the night

As we sat in the van in Thessaloniki University waiting for the gig to start, people started to walk past the van in the direction of the venue. People just kept coming, it was reaching biblical proportions. We didn't know where the fuck they were going but it must have been something big. As it neared show-time we were amazed to discover they were all going to the gig. The place was a college refectory and probably managed to squeeze in about four hundred people, but it had big doors along the side that opened out into a courtyard, and there must have been over a thousand people all together. Fires were being lit and the whole scene was somewhat mind blowing. Zounds are quite big in Greece so I guess I shouldn't have been that surprised. Unfortunately the equipment for the show was terrible. An awful P.A. that buzzed and hummed and broke down intermittently. The stage was small and crowded with the useless support band's equipment. We started playing and it sounded awful. I kept breaking strings. I tried to use the guitar of the support band, but the asshole that owned it came up on stage and took it off me. We went down really well, but it was not because we were any good, we were shit and I was distraught. All that effort to get down there, undergoing sleep deprivation and tortuous drives, just to fuck up in front of a huge crowd that had been waiting years to see us.

Then to top it all, after we played, I thought I'd go for a walk to chill out a bit. As I wandered away from the venue I was met by a big crowd of people rushing back towards the hall and shouting. There was a bitter smell in the air and I could taste something strange on my tongue. Someone told me that a large proportion of the crowd were out on the street rioting and setting fire to cars, consequently the police were firing tear gas into the University to quell the rioters. 'Was it something I said' I enquired.

'No' came the reply, 'it is a public holiday and the Greeks like to riot. The police are not allowed onto university property so the rioters are running back in here and the police are firing teargas into the place'. It made the national TV news, but thankfully we weren't implicated!

The Athens of Greece

Next stop was Athens, and this was completely different. We were met by a driver/minder who was moonlighting from his regular job as a police officer. We were offered anything we wanted, legal or illegal. We stayed in hotels, were driven to radio interviews and generally treated like rock stars. We played at the An Club, the place was sold out, the sound system fantastic and for once we managed to turn in a great set at a prestigious gig, something all incarnations of Zounds would consistently fail at. After the glory that was Greece it was another monster drive to Skopje in Macedonia, where we encountered more poverty and hardship. Then we got up at some ridiculous hour to drive eight hours from Skopje to Zagreb in Croatia.

More trouble at the border

In the end it turned out to be a lot longer than eight hours, more like eighteen in fact. We got to the customs post between Macedonia and Serbia and we were ordered to drive into a compound for lorries and wait. We waited. As we waited we could see groups of Serbian customs officials opening up all the lorries and helping themselves to the contents. Not loads of stuff, but something for everyone. I suppose it was an unofficial tax.

Protag, who was doing most of the driving, and who owned the van, was ordered over to an office. He explained that we were a band on our way to a show in Zagreb and we were not stopping in Serbia. They said we had to pay a transit tax in order to transport our equipment through the country. We phoned Serbian friends and they informed us there was no such tax. The border patrol didn't care what our friends said, either we paid the tax or things would get a lot more difficult. After having been kept around for two to three hours we were in danger of missing the show in Zagreb. We were forced to pay. It cost us pretty much all the money we had. They also said that in order to prevent us from stopping in Serbia, and selling our equipment, we would have to have a police officer riding in the van with us to the Croatian border. The cop was a young guy who looked nervous and didn't speak English. We stopped at a service station and bought him a coffee. The only words he could muster as he raised his arms in mock desperation were 'Serbia, crazy Serbia'.

We stopped at more services near Belgrade and picked up our friend Maja who wanted a lift to Zagreb. She got in and furiously started to harangue our police escort. He looked sheepish and didn't put up much of a defence. Maja informed us that he knew we were a band engaged in legitimate business, he knew we were not going to try to sell the equipment in Serbia, he was aware that we had been ripped off and forced to pay a tax that didn't exist, he was embarrassed by the whole thing and hoped we didn't feel too badly about him or his country. By the time he left us, later that night at the Croatian border, we were like old pals, shaking hands, slapping each other on the back, smiling and waving profusely.

We got to the Zagreb gig really late and played around midnight. Damo Suzuki of Can was supposed to play and we could have joined him on stage, but he never made it due to a French airport workers strike. Annoying for me because I love Damo, and on three separate occasions I have had the chance to play with him, something has thwarted it.

The tour continued through Germany. I collapsed after the gig in Stuttgart and freaked out the local hippies by carving the words 'Sturm und Drang' into their kitchen table. I didn't realise it was such a bad thing. But then I was fucked up and there was certainly 'Sturm und Drang' going on in my head.

After three tortuous weeks on the emotional seesaw that is life-on-tour, it finally ground to a halt in a small town in Belgium. We had been hired by a load of ex-punk rockers that in the intervening years had become lawyers and estate agents and all manner of professionals. They had booked us as a nostalgia novelty act, to play at a sort of glorified high-school reunion event in an art centre. It was humiliating. The only good thing was that we had hotels booked for the night with showers and TVs and breakfast. Except it was Protag's turn to go off the rails again, and he insisted we drive back to London straight after the gig. We were shattered and in no condition to do anything other than sleep. We pointed this out to him. We tried to impress upon him the folly and the danger of falling asleep at the wheel and careering off the road on what would be an all night drive. None of us would be able to endure it, least of all him. Nothing would sway him though, and the rest of us were too weak and gave up the fight.

We limped back to London. They let me out and somehow continued on to Bradford. We had one more gig booked at the Solfest in Solway Firth. We all turned up separately and played really well to an enthusiastic crowd, most of whom probably knew nothing about us. During the set loads of toddlers and young kids came up on stage to stage-dive into their parents' arms. Blyth Power had been on before us so Joseph came up and sang 'Dancing' with us, which was appropriate. There was a nice symmetry to that, as not only was he reunited with Zounds, but also with Protag, who had been a central pillar of Blyth Power for so many years. Protag retired from music after that gig. I said I had had enough and was putting the band to rest again, and that was it for a few years.

The Redemption Of Zounds

Feeding Of The 5000 - Zounds eternal -
A big fuck off to the punk police

Feeding Of The 5000 Shepherd's Bush gig

I decided to get Zounds back together for a gig at the Shepherd's Bush Empire in London. The gig featured us, and a load of other second division bands associated with the Crass label. We were all supporting original Crass singer Steve Ignorant and friends performing 'The Feeding Of The 5000', the Crass' debut album. It went over 2 nights and was considered either

A complete sell-out of everything the bands involved ever believed in, where ageing, brain addled, weak minded, has-beens paraded their in-flated egos and tired bodies for one last shot at a bit of glory and nice pay day;

Or

A cracking weekend where a load of tremendous, rarely seen bands played for a fair price and performed material that a lot of people loved and hadn't seen in many years, and in many cases never seen at all.

The truth, as always, was somewhere between the two. The punk police were always going to hate it. They are generally not into the music but more into a particular ethos. I see where they are coming from and am not unsympathetic. But I am also a musician in a band, and I need to play to eat and feed my habits. No one got ripped off, no one was forced to go, and no one made a fortune (that I am aware of).

It's a great venue to see a band, but it is a shit venue to play. We were treated in a perfunctory manner by the sound crew, who seemed to think they were the most important people there. We were treated like shit by the venue staff and security, whose job seemed to be to act as unpleasantly and unhelpfully as possible. Zounds got paid £400, which as we were a four -piece at the time, is not a great deal of money once you've spent time in a rehearsal room and sorted out transport.

After that we started to get more offers of gigs and I just thought, fuck it, I want to play the guitar really loud and sing my songs to people so why not. I had picked up a brilliant rhythm section in bass-devil Paul 'overdose' O'Donnell and drummer Paul Gilbert. Sadly all the songs I wrote originally for Zounds are still relevant today, and probably will be for a long time. I've written a load of new ones which we recorded in 2010/11. This slightly undermines my idea that bands should only record one album. But fuck it, I felt like it. Who cares if the purists think it is devaluing the original intention. We had to have punk rock in the first place to get rid of that sort of thinking. In fact the band didn't even have an original intention beyond the fact we wanted to play music, have fun and get stoned. Weirdly, after all these years, those are still my main aims. So, I will never disband Zounds again. And we will make loads more records.

It doesn't matter if you're beautiful or ugly, able-bodied or disabled, gay or straight, black or white, young or old. If you want to do it don't let anyone tell you not to. As the Pink Fairies sang all those years ago, 'Don't think about it, all you got to do is do it'! Punk is dead, long live punk and a big fuck off to the punk police.

28 CRY GENIE CRY

I was born into a world that I didn't create
The nurse smacked my arse and she told me to wait
She said that one day it would all become clear
So I waited and I waited I'm still waiting to hear
They all gathered round and they stared at me
And some speculated what one day I would be
Will he be famous or a great engineer
Will he be straight well I hope he's not queer

Because I still don't know what I'm supposed to be
I still don't know what I'm supposed to be
I still don't know what I'm supposed to be
I don't know what I'm supposed to be

They took me back home and it came time for school
Sending me there was bewildering and cruel
They sat on your hands if you tried to have fun
If you spoke out of turn then they'd cut out your tongue
I can't give up coffee, sugar or tea
I can't give up sex and it won't give up me
I can't give up anger though I've tried and I've tried
Cos I'm aching and I'm hurting and I'm crying inside

Because I still don't know what I'm supposed to be
I still don't know what I'm supposed to be
I still don't know what I'm supposed to be
I don't know what I'm supposed to be

I don't want enemies but I can't pretend
I don't have a few and some use to be friends
I want to be good and to live like a saint
But I guess I'm too twisted and I ain't got the patience
I railed and I raged but they kept the door shut
She said it seems that you're bigger but you never grew up
Emotionally retarded so cry baby cry
I said you're heartless she said fuck off and die

Because I still don't know what I'm supposed to be
I still don't know what I'm supposed to be
I still don't know what I'm supposed to be
I don't know what I'm supposed to be

29 SUPERMARCHE

It's Christmas in the supermarket and everything's so cheap
Let's go down there and get our share because it might
not be for keeps
Nice Indian boys make colourful toys to keep the shelves
well stocked
It must be grim to have to be him but at least he's got a job

The bankers take a holiday and find somewhere to go
Some dark nights it just seems right to keep the profile low
The instigators claim that now they've renounced all
their crimes.
So they're laying back and taking the flak but they're
just biding their time

The discontent went and pitched their tents in the middle
of the square
They began to sing and declaim that things could be a
little more fair
The security force was deployed of course to keep the
rabble down
They did what they did and kept their numbers hid cos
they're the biggest gang in town

Things can only get better
All the candidates would say
But it didn't take long till it all went wrong
And we're where we are today
I start to slip and I lose my grip
And my mind drifts back to war
The master's doing nicely thank you
While the poor just kill the poor

30 MAKE LOVE NOT WAR

Why do people have to hurt each other
Act mean and ugly and nasty to each other
Set brother 'gainst sister, sister 'gainst brother
Why do people have to hurt each other

Make love not war

I can't work out why people keep fighting
Keep screaming and screeching and scratching and biting
Everybody's hating and their baiting and inciting
I just don't know why people keep fighting

Make love not war

I don't want to die for you
I don't want you to die for me
I don't want to kill for you
I don't want you to kill for me

Why do people push each other to the limit
They're fighting over something when there's really
nothing in it
It's something and nothing you really should forget it
But you've got your foolish pride so someone's gonna get it

Mummy
My brother and I
We've been fighting again
We had sticks for guns
Mummy
My sister and I
We've been quarrelling again
We had sticks for tongues

Mummy
There's a man down the street
He says there are other men
Who want to be mean to me
Mummy
There's a voice on the screen
He wants me to fight for the cause
I think that he's lying to me

It's just another roadside attraction
It's just another spectacular situation
I sit here watching it on widescreen television
And the more I see it oh the harder it is to feel

Mummy
They've put the war on television
It's spectacular and interesting
All the pretty colours
Mummy
There are people in the jungle
There are people in the desert
They're dying of starvation

32 WHAT MAKES A MAN A MAN TODAY (slight return)

What makes a man a man today
What makes him say the things he say
What makes a woman act in the way
A woman acts in the world today

Who put all of those thoughts inside of my head
Who put all of that language in the books that I read
Who decides who starves and who gets fed
Who put all of those things inside of my head

All the types outside my door
Look like me less or more
But I don't know if they think like me
Or if I'm just some kind of freak
I don't know what people believe
I don't know if they think like me
I don't know what colours they see
Or if they see the things I see

What makes a man woman man
What makes his arms and legs and hands
Do all the things that they do
What makes them move the way they move
Is my mind free or is it bound by all the things that I
found
Before I came unto this place before I face the things I
face

All the types outside my door
Look like me less or more
But I don't know if they think like me
Or if I'm just some kind of freak
I don't know what people believe
I don't know if they think like me
I don't know what colours they see
Or if they see the things I see

Is it the place that I was born
Is it my time in history
Is it the parents that I had

Is it the magazines I read
Is it the woman on TV
Is it the films upon my wall
Is it the shadows in the night
Is it the teachers from my school

33 WHAT IS IT WORTH

When the hurricane screams and the levee breaks
And the flood comes in and the buildings shake
Lovers are parted as the city quakes
What people build up Mother Nature can take
You lose your soul to gain the earth
You lose your soul so what is it worth
You lose your soul then you lose the earth
You lose your soul so what is it worth

What is it worth when the hammer comes down
What is it worth when the wheel goes round
What have you lost that can't be found
What is it worth when the hammer comes down

You can have faith in all that stuff
You worked for and bought and learnt to love
But what is it worth when it's covered in mud
Scattered over miles by the raging flood

Money goes soft and the bank gets tough
The work dries up and the going gets rough
In pastures of plenty there is never enough
You're running on empty while a few are stuffed

34 DAMAGE

Not sure who I am talking to
Is there anybody out there at all
This is dedicated to anyone
Who feels as disposed as I do

I don't want to be a part
Of the hurt that people cause
To everything and to each other
Over land and sea and shore
Don't feel part of anything
Done in anybody's name
I'm not proud of who I am
But I am not ashamed

I don't belong to anyone
I don't belong to anything
I'm like an island in this world
Don't know if I will sink or swim

Who knows if there'll ever come a time
When all the damage that's been done
To every living thing on earth
Will be made right and be undone

I don't want to be a part
Of the hurt that people cause
To everything and to each other
Over land and sea and shore
Don't feel part of anything
Done in anybody's name
I'm not proud of who I am
But I am not ashamed

I don't belong to anyone
I don't belong to anything
I'm like an island in this world
Don't know if I will sink or swim

35 FOLLOW THE MONEY

This one looks at that one
That one's talking back
Another one looks nervous
And someone starts to crack
It's hard to tell the good ones
Tell them from the bad
It's hard to face the future
When you have to watch your back

Follow all the money
See where it stops
Trace it on its journey
From the bottom to the top
It starts in the gutter
And rises up like fat
It rises up like cream and
It's never coming back

Take a look around and see who's got a future round here
Scratch each others back and you start to advance your career
From the bottom of the pile to the great and the good on high
Everybody's complicit with the big lie

Down on the corner
Out in the street
Everything's on offer
From fresh dope to dead meat
Look at all the pennies
You and everybody spent
You ended up with nothing
And you wonder where it went

Everyone's an expert
And they got a point of view
And everybody wonders why
Nobody else thinks like they do
They all make presumptions
About what's going on
They all make predictions
But they always turn out wrong

M-O-N-E-Y

36 DEPORTEE

I come from a place that I call home
That year the rains refused to come
That year the crops refused to grow
The kids were sick when I left home
There was no work there to be done
There was some money that I owed
I had no option but to go
To go somewhere to make some dough

I come from Mexico, I come from Vietnam
From Albania and from Kazakhstan
I nearly died at sea, and I was robbed on land
I didn't want to go but what choice did I have

They called me immigrant and refugee
They called me criminal and stared at me
And now I know what it is I will be
All I will be, is Deportee

I came upon these city walls
Waiting for all the cards to fall
But I was getting nothing at all
Except the curse of one and all
I did a bit of this and a bit of that
Made some pennies selling cigarettes
Biding my time and laying low
Until the time I'm forced to go

Got your finger got your face
Got your blood type on a trace
Got your number got your name
Got it time and time again
Know the hours on your clock
The combination to your lock
Know where it is you have been
And when you're gonna go again

Everything's in place for the clampdown honey
Everything's in place just in case of something
Got nothing to hide they say you got no worry
But I feel a bit uneasy cos I feel there's something

Know the numbers on your phone
When you're out and when you're home
When you sleep and when you feed
The kind of books you like to read
Know the groceries that you choose
And how much paper that you use
What makes you happy and makes you blue
Your history and what you'll do

They know the books you like to read
And what you dream when you're asleep
They know the things you like to do
The people you like to do it to

38 ANCIENT BRITON

I'm an ancient Briton I was born to fight
I was born to get pissed on a Friday night
I was born to be sick on the town hall steps
I don't take prisoners and I don't take lip

I'm an ancient Briton I'm the king of clubs
Two world wars and one world cup
Made out of curry, lager and blood
I'm going down the football then I'll see you down the
pub

Ancient Briton what you gonna do

I'm an ancient Briton I can make fresh tracks
I've been to Real Zaragoza and deported back
But I'm not bothered, give me some slack
I'll be as right as rain when I've had a kebab

I'm an ancient Briton I was born to text
Pictures of women's breasts and legs
I've got them on my phone as a load of mpegs
Cos I'm always too drunk to find any sex

Ancient Briton what you gonna do

Two world wars, one world cup
We can't play like Brazil but they can't drink like us
Two world wars, one world cup
We can't play like Brazil but they can't drink like us

Ancient Briton what you gonna do

39 Sick Of Work

I picked up the phone and called in sick to the boss
I could tell he didn't believe me but I couldn't give a
toss
Made my voice a little feeble and he sounded quite cross
But when I put the phone down I just laughed it off

There's some black kids smiling in a flat on the estate
They're having lots of fun because they're mixing drum
and bass
There's some white kids laughing 'cos they've had a
little spliff
Playing in the garage stealing Rolling Stones riffs

I'm not going to work today
The sun is out and I wanna say
Hello I love you won't you have a nice day
I'm not going to work today

I'm not sick I'm just sick of work
The people there are nice enough but sometimes they get
on my nerves
I'm not sick I'm just sick of work
I'll wander down the avenue and have a cup of tea with
you
I'm not sick I'm just sick of work
It's not that I don't like the job but then again maybe it is
I'm not sick I'm just sick of work

I might lay in bed a while then soak in the bath
Wander down the avenue have coffee in the park
Go to a museum, take in a little art
Sit and watch youtube while I'm playing my guitar

Do a little shopping, pick up some DVDs
Sit and eat some ice cream while I'm watching the TV
Start to write my novel or just hang out with friends
So much stuff tomorrow I might blow out work again

I'm not going to work today
The sun is out and I wanna say

Hello I love you won't you have a nice day
I'm not going to work today

I'm not sick I'm just sick of work
The people there are nice enough but sometimes they just
piss me off
I'm not sick I'm just sick of work
I'll wander down the avenue and have a cup of tea with
you
I'm not sick I'm just sick of work
It's not that I don't like the job but then again maybe it is
I'm not sick I'm just sick of work

Looking at the symbols painted on my wall - Brougham Road in the 1980s

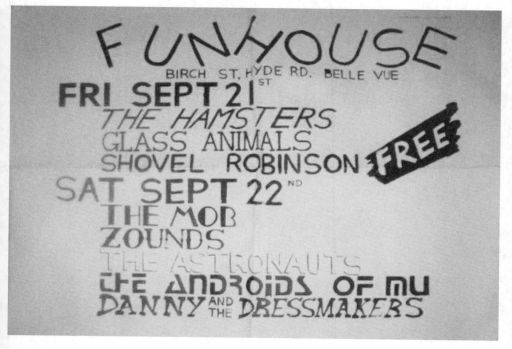

Weird Tales go to Manchester for the first time.

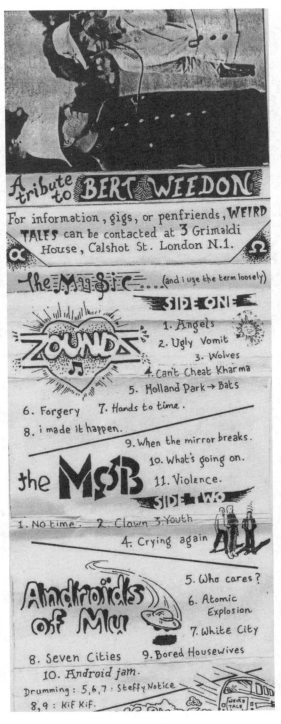

A tribute to BERT WEEDON

For information, gigs, or penfriends, WEIRD TALES can be contacted at 3 Grimaldi House, Calshot St. London N.1.

the Music .... (and i use the term loosely)

SIDE ONE

ZOUNDS

1. Angels
2. Ugly Vomit
3. Wolves
4. Can't Cheat Kharma
5. Holland Park → Bats
6. Forgery   7. Hands to time.
8. i made it happen.
9. When the mirror breaks.
10. What's going on.

the MOB

11. Violence.

SIDE TWO

1. No time.   2. Clown 3. Youth
4. Crying again

Androids of Mu

5. Who cares?
6. Atomic Explosion
7. White City
8. Seven Cities   9. Bored Housewives
10. Android jam.
Drumming: 5,6,7: Steffy Notice
8,9: Kif Kif.

Weird Tales compilation tape.

144

Poster for the first Weird Tales tour.

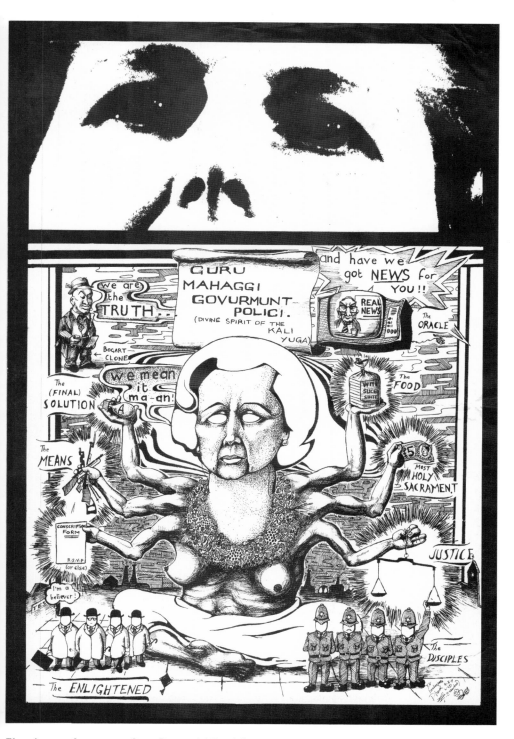

The banned cover for Demystification.

Not sure this gig ever took place.

Low life in the low countries

Hendersonville 2011 - I keep a close watch

Keep on rockin' in the free world

Discography

Can't Cheat Karma/ War/ Subvert. 1980 UK 7" (Crass - 421984/3)

Demystification/ Great White Hunter. 1981 UK 7" (Rough Trade - RT 069)

The Curse Of Zounds. 1981 UK LP (Rough Trade - ROUGH 31)
Fear/ Did He Jump Or Was He Pushed/ The Unfree Child/ My Mummy's
Gone/ Little Bit More/ This Land/ New Band/ Dirty Squatters/ Loads
Of Noise/ Target/ Mr. Disney/The War Drags On

Dancing/ True Love. March 1982 UK 7"
(Rough Trade - RT 094)

More Trouble Coming Every Day/ Knife. Aug 1982 UK 7"
(Rough Trade - RT 098)

La Vache Qui Rit EP. 1983 Belgium 7" (Not So Brave - NSB 001)
Not Me/ Biafra/ Fear/ Wolves 1983 Belgium

Singles Compilation Vinyl LP 1983
(Base Records Italy)

This Land/ Alone 2001 UK 7" and CD single
(McLabel/Rugger Bugger/Active - MCLABEL 1/DUMP 51/ACTIVE 2)

This Land/ Alone 2001 UK 7" and CD single
(McLabel/Rugger Bugger/Active - MCLABEL 1/DUMP 51/ACTIVE 2)

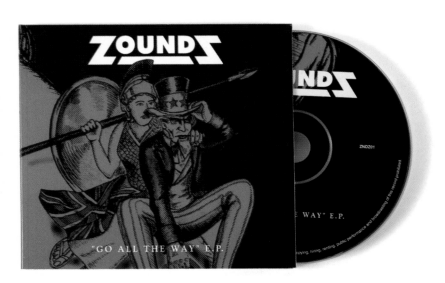

Go All The Way. 2005 Belgium CD (ZNDZ - ZNDZ 01 Digi-pack)
Go All The Way/ War Fever/ Kamp America

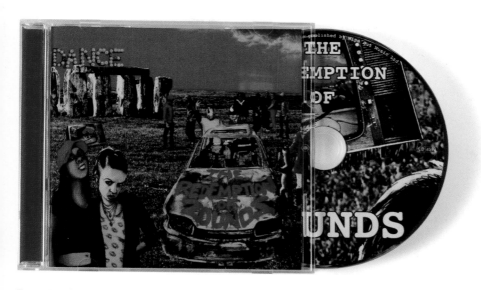

Zounds 'The Redemption Of Zounds' July 2011 LP
Overground - OVER 128CD USA vinyl Broken Rekids
Cry Genie CrySupermarcheMake Love Not WarAnother Roadside
AttractionWhat Makes a Man a Man Today (Slight Return)What Is It
WorthDamageFollow The Money DeporteeWaiting For the Clampdown Honey

Ancient Briton / Sick of work UK 7" single
(Overground - OVER133)

Singles & EPs 1980-1984
(5x7", RE + Box, Comp)
2011 Broken Rekids

PHOTOS BY
Mickey 'Penguin' Baxter.
Val Drayton

Published by Active Distribution
All copyright and rights held by Steve Lake.

SUB-EDITOR
Kevin Sheridan

DESIGN
Onno Hesselink

Characters (accomplices, victims and bystanders)

Laurence Wood, Joseph Porter, Tim Hutton, Brian Pugsley, Jonathan Barnett, Kif Kif La Dobson, Grant Showbiz, Phil the Terrible, Mark Astronaut, Geoff Travis, Gina Raincoat, Judge, Shanks, Pete Synth, Kevin Sheridan, Captain Max, Steve Burch, Jimmy Lacie, Nick Godwin, Protag, Mickey Dread, Brad Grisdale, Adam Kidron, Mark, Curtis and Graham Mob, Onno, Steve and Alison Retford, Jon Active, Colchester Steve Hyland, Jimdog, Stick, Bryan Swirsky, Dave Burokas, Mike Costarella, Dave Ed, Jason Willer, Greg Ingraham, Mike Millett, Sean Forbes, John Esplen, Mike Thornberry, Gary Durham, Eastfield, Mandy, Milli, Gabbi, Jake